A HUNDRED AND ONE THINGS TO DO

WEST SEATTLE 101

A HUNDRED AND ONE THINGS TO DO

WEST SEATTLE 101

An Insider's Guide to Recreation, Dining, Entertainment & Enrichment

LORI HINTON

Adventure Press

Seattle, Washington

West Seattle 101: A Hundred and One Things to Do

© 2005 by Lori Hinton

Copyeditor: Emily Bedard
Cover: Vintage Volvo wagon near Alki Beach
Design: Peter D'Agostino and Allison Kline
Illustration: Damon Brown
Maps: Peter D'Agostino
Photography: Mike Hipple

ISBN: 1-881583-11-2

Adventure Press
P.O. Box 14059
Seattle, Washington 98114
206.200.2578 (v) 206.568.0592 (f)
adventurepress.com

Adventure Press books are printed in the U.S. on recycled paper.

Disclaimer: As is the nature of any guidebook, the information within this book is subject to change. Before you plan your day around any one of the following 101 Things to Do, please call or check suggested websites to confirm that hours of operation and other vital stats still hold true.

Second Printing

Acknowledgments

This book is dedicated to my home—to every friendly person, tail-wagging dog and treasured tree—you all make this a deeply cherished place to be. Thank you, West Seattle, for inspiring me to write about you.

Thank you, Scott Matual, for being my prized partner, the president of my unofficial book support group and willing companion in my continual quest to discover new things to do in our own backyard.

Thank you, Hinton fam (and Hobie), for the walks in Lincoln Park and for bringing me up in an active, encouraging environment.

Thank you, Jack Mayne and the *West Seattle Herald*, for your insight in hiring me to write my "101 Things to Do in West Seattle" column, the source of much of this content.

And to the book crew, thank you. To John Zilly for your sage advice and readiness to take on the project and see it through. Thanks, Mike Hipple, for your energy and enthusiasm in capturing the essence of our little Mayberry with your amazing photography. Thank you, Emily Bedard, Damon Brown, Peter D'Agostino, and Allison Kline, for your contributions in talent and time. Thanks to Philip Shaw and 100 Cameras, for helping get *West Seattle 101* off the ground.

And thank you, all my West Seattle family and friends—your love, support, and appreciation for "all things good" in the neighborhood lights my way. Thank you, thank you!

Contents

Foreword by Bill Nye

Walking in West Seattle, you don't have to worry about asking directions. People there are happy to show you around. West Seattleites don't just like West Seattle—they love it. And no wonder. West Seattle is a special place. It's part of one of the world's most livable cities, but in its own zone—a little bit isolated, a little bit quirky. It's hard to get there without riding a big ol' bridge or an old road that has just enough hills, corners, and potholes to keep West Seattle off the beaten path. And Lori Hinton is the perfect gal to show you around ("gal" being the West Seattle way to say "charming woman").

I met Lori when we were both working on a TV show in Seattle, and I could tell right away that she had a comfort that comes from growing up in the West Seattle scene. Most of the scenes are stunning vistas. But the scene? It's ingrained. See, people don't leave West Seattle. The neighborhood and the people are soul mates. I've crossed the big bridge countless times in search of fresh bread, fabulous fish, and an amazing place to swim. There's fly fishing in the surf and kite flying on the beach with skyscrapers and salmon fisheries as a backdrop. I recommend spending some time among the only ancient, un-cut, old-growth trees in the city. It may be the only old-growth forest any of us will ever visit. West Seattleites get all this without leaving home.

In *West Seattle 101*, Lori shares West Seattle with us. Take her advice, and you'll do business with folks whose ancestors settled there generations ago. People like Lori have traveled, seen a great deal of the world, but they come home to live. Whether you are already part of West Seattle or are curious about it, do yourself a favor and try a few of these 101 things yourself. You'll meet your neighbors, make some new friends, eat some great food, and have a blast along the way. There's lots to do.

West Seattle isn't just a good place to do things; it's a great place to just be. Let Lori be your guide. I guarantee you'll live it up, West Seattle-style.

March 17, 2005

Introduction

West Seattle 101 is an eclectic collection of 101 different things to do in West Seattle, Washington—from kite surfing off Alki Beach to indulging in Husky Deli's famous ice cream. A guidebook for a neighborhood that's like a town of its own, *West Seattle 101* features outdoor and indoor adventures, favorite restaurants and out-of-the-way haunts, fine arts and distinctively different diversions, enriching education and inspiring ideas for self-improvement. It also includes a peek at the pioneers that make up this diverse peninsula and mini-histories on how these 101 things came to be.

Much like a trusty travel guide with a little bit of attitude, *West Seattle 101* serves up slightly quirky, activity-oriented stories—each with a detailed, easy-access information box so that readers have everything they need to know right at their fingertips.

Providing "undiscovered" activities for neighborhood veterans as well as a virtual stockpile of activities for newcomers or out-of-town tourists (even those traveling from just across the bridge)—*West Seattle 101* is a must-have for Westside natives and visitors alike.

Dave McCoy of Emerald Water Anglers fly fishes for sea-run cutthroat off Lowman Beach.

RECREATION

Surrounded by Puget Sound on three sides, West Seattle is a playground for adventurers. Whether you opt for adrenaline by kite surfing off Alki or you prefer the mellower, more sentimental tradition of gathering around a beach bonfire to welcome the Christmas ship, you'll find 27 different indoor and outdoor adventures right here.

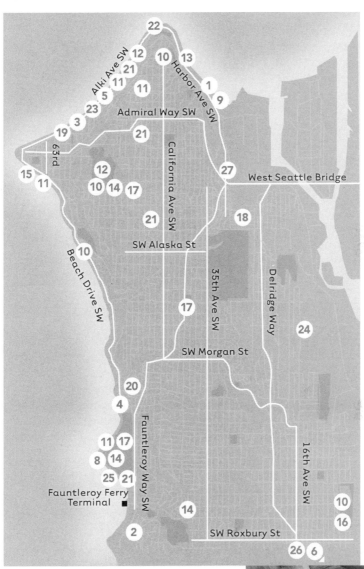

Alki Ave SW

22

12 · 10 · 13

21

11 · 1 · 9

5

23

Admiral Way SW

3

19

21

63rd

15

11

12

California Ave SW

27 West Seattle Bridge

10 · 14 · 17

18

21

SW Alaska St

35th Ave SW

Delridge Way

10

Beach Drive SW

17

24

SW Morgan St

20

4

Fauntleroy Way SW

11 · 17

8 · 14

16th Ave SW

10

25 · 21

16

Fauntleroy Ferry
Terminal ■

14

2

SW Roxbury St

26 · 6

RECREATION

1 | Take a Kayak Trek

Ever experienced the wetter side of West Seattle? Discover a whole new world of wildlife and sea-level scenery when you paddle a kayak around the peninsula and see West Seattle from the water side.

Harbor seals, salmon, and heron will keep you company along the way. And if you're lucky, you may even spot a bald eagle. Head down to Seacrest Marina, just steps from Salty's on Alki, for an amazing outdoor experience.

> *Harbor seals, salmon, and heron will keep you company along the way.*

You can take a guided tour with Alki Kayak Tours or rent kayaks by the hour from Alki Crab & Fish Co.

The tours depart from the Seacrest Boathouse at various times and on various days from May through October, so be sure to call Alki Kayak Tours to reserve your spot. Trips range from the shorter 2-hour Sunset Paddle to the half-day Alki Lighthouse Tour and the Blake Island Overnight. For beginning boaters or paddlers looking for helpful tips, safety instruction, and interesting information on natural history, this is the way to go.

For do-it-yourselfers, single and double kayaks are available for rent by the hour and include paddles and PFDs (personal flotation devices). A 1-hour trip will give you a taste for kayaking, but allow a few hours for more in-depth exploring.

Fair-weather paddlers will want to get a jump on kayaking in the months where summer sun provides extra warmth atop the cool water breeze. But for seasoned West Seattleites, kayak treks bring happiness rain or shine. Many fancy a morning or midday trek on the weekend (or a day playing hooky) and sunset paddles are a beautiful way to end the day.

But the weather changes as often as the tide, so make sure to bring warm clothing (water-wicking fleece or wool recommended), a hat (long brims help with glare), sunglasses, sun block, a whistle, and a water bottle (full, of course). And for wildlife viewing, don't forget binoculars and a laminated copy of *Mac's Field Guide to Puget Sound*, if you please.

Taking a kayak trek on your own for the first time? A popular route is a roundtrip paddle to the Alki lighthouse. Adventurous boaters have also paddled as far as Puget Sound's outlying islands. On longer treks, a beach break is a great way to refuel and stretch your legs. Pack a lunch or grab an order of fish and chips to go from Alki Crab & Fish Co. before hopping in your streamlined craft.

So take a tour or splash around solo. Either way, boating in Elliott Bay will give you a new perspective on West Seattle and the abundant marine life that surrounds this picturesque peninsula.

What:
Sea Kayaking

Where:
Seacrest Marina
Alki Crab & Fish Co.
1660 Harbor Avenue SW
206.938.0975

Alki Kayak Tours
www.kayakalki.com
206.953.0237

When:
Year-round. Hours change by the season; call ahead to check.

Price:
Alki Kayak Tours:
Sunset Paddle $39
Alki Lighthouse Tour $49
Duwamish River $49
Blake Island Overnight $149

Alki Crab & Fish Co. Rentals:
$15/hour for singles
$25/hour for doubles
Call for details

2 | Welcome Back, Coho

Each year glorious orange and red leaves fall. Favorite hats are put back into circulation and the excitement of beginning a brand new year (in the school sense) begins.

And from roughly Halloween to Thanksgiving, there's also something special that happens out in the Sound and at a certain stream right beneath West Seattle residents' wool-sock-wearing feet.

The West Seattle community awaits with open arms and open eyes for coho salmon to return to Fauntleroy Creek.

"The fish are as much a part of the Fauntleroy community as the people who live here," smiles creek advocate and Fauntleroy Watershed Council executive Judy Pickens.

Built in 1998 by Seattle Public Utilities, a viewpoint, a culvert, and a fish ladder were established to aid salmon returning to mile-long Fauntleroy Creek. Annual fish counts in recent years have varied from as few as five to nearly 200.

Be one of the first to witness this miracle of life when you stop by Fauntleroy Creek to see the spawners.

"Each year, we begin to see fish school in the cove, fisherman at the park say the fish stop biting—which is a sign they are preparing to spawn—and the creek is ready for returning fish," explains Pickens.

Besides strolling by and seeing the fish for yourself, there are several ways to dabble in the neighborhood's fish fever festivities each fall.

> "The fish are as much a part of the Fauntleroy community as the people who live here."
>
> Judy Pickens
> Fauntleroy Watershed Council executive

Call the Salmon Home with a Drum Ceremony
Come to the fish-ladder viewpoint and join the joyful community of salmon supporters in the annual "Call Our Salmon Home" drumming ceremony.

"The drumming ceremony has become a real community event," says Pickens.

The ceremony includes art, storytelling, songs, and a drum circle. Bring a drum (if you've got one) and dress for the weather.

"This is a simple way to give people a sense of participating," encourages Pickens. "Just being able to walk a few blocks, push your baby buggies, bring your teenagers, and have fun."

Be a Salmon Watcher

You can also grab a front row seat on the creek by volunteering to count returning fish. Watchers of all ages are welcome. All you need are a good set of eyes, a little bit of free time to spend in nature, and an interest in learning more about the magical creatures that swim in the waters around you. Training is provided and the watch runs from the end of October until Thanksgiving (or for as long as there are fish). For more information contact Sherry Richardson at 206.935.8981.

What:
Spawning Silvers

Where:
Fauntleroy Creek
(across from the ferry dock on Fauntleroy Way SW)
www.fauntleroy.net
206.938.4203

When:
Timing is critical.
The spawning season in Fauntleroy Creek runs roughly between late October and mid-late November.

Price:
Free

Embark on a Fish-full Field Trip

Educate and fascinate kids and adults alike with a field trip to Fauntleroy Creek. Guided field trips are great for classes, special organizations, families, or anyone interested in learning about the fantastic finned creatures of Fauntleroy. For field trip information, call Judy Pickens at 206.932.4203.

3 | Build a Beach Bonfire on Alki

When summer hits Alki, it's hard not to notice the scene. Lowriders thump in the background while bikers, runners and Roller-bladers all try not to collide.

The place is like a mini Venice Beach during the wild summer days. But when the sun goes down and the cool night air settles, a different and oftentimes tranquil Alki returns, even if only for a few hours.

Bonfires beckon soul-searchers and those who simply enjoy the primitive pleasure of staring deep into the fire for hours on end.

And there's no better time for a blazing beach bonfire.

When night falls, bonfires beckon soul-searchers and those who simply enjoy the primitive pleasure of staring deep into the fire for hours on end. The reflective nature of gathering around a bonfire to watch the dancing flames provides a kind of comfort that can be hard to come by in the city.

But West Seattleites are lucky because Seattle Parks and Recreation picked this neighborhood beach to receive a handful of giant fire pits for all to enjoy. You'll feel like you're out at a remote coastal beach, but you're just across the bay from the city.

Do note that fires are allowed only in the designated fire pits and are available on a first-come, first-serve basis. In fact, Alki bonfire-building professionals often stake their claim even before sunset. But if you are willing to be an extrovert and join in on someone else's flame, fire-watchers will often-times share the warmth. Bringing s'mores as a peace offering might do the trick. Just don't let the seagulls steal your bright idea the minute you turn your back.

Once you get in the swing of the bonfire thing, you may even want to start carrying a "bonfire kit" in the back of your rig or mount one to your bike for those spontaneous moments when busting out a fire sounds fun. Just load up a milk crate with the essentials—a few dry logs, kindling, newspaper, and a lighter—and you're good to go.

Although summer is prime time, bonfires can ignite year-round enjoyment. It's amazing how warm they can keep you on an otherwise unbearably chilly night.

It is said that this same site on Alki Beach is where Chief Seattle greeted the first European settlers on a cold, stormy day in 1851. Bet they wished the bonfire pits were roaring back then.

What:
Beach Bonfire

Where:
Alki Beach (on the wide, sandy stretch of beach between 59th & 56th)
Alki Ave SW
206.684.4075

When:
Year-round

Price:
Free; BYOW (bring your own wood—and matches of, course)

4 | Fly Fish Westside Waters

Outdoors. Close to home. Surrounded by fish. What could be better than walking the beach, wading in the waves, and catching a few finned creatures?

Not much, assures local fly fishing guide Mark Freda of Emerald Water Anglers.

"I do saltwater walk and wade trips in West Seattle," smiles Freda. "And none of that needs a boat. Just walking and wading."

Anglers can fish off Lincoln Park, on Lowman Beach, or near the Southworth Ferry Dock—minutes from any home on the Westside, providing more time watching your line in the water and less time traveling to far-off watersheds.

Upon arrival at the beach, the first step is tying on the right fly for the right species during the right time of year. But don't worry—your guide will help you decide. He'll even take a photo of you and your first fish if you ask.

So what type of fish are we talking here?

> "We go for sea-run cutthroats, silver salmon, pinks and chum."
>
> Mark Freda
> fly fishing guide

"We go for sea-run cutthroats, silver salmon, pinks, and chum," says Freda.

Summertime is prime time for most species. From August through October you'll find coho or silver salmon weighing in at up to 15 pounds. Chum arrive in late summer, and every odd-numbered year the pinks come around, too.

But fathom this: Sea-run cutthroat, or "cuts," are fishable all year long. Although, according to Freda, you're "luckier" in August as the cuts prepare to spawn and congregate in large groups near banks and streams. Thanks to the geography (and a little West Seattle karma), the neighborhood is perfectly set up for this species.

West Seattle features miles of saltwater shorelines, most of which is public beach accessible to all. Small creeks flow into the Sound, providing freshwater resources that are veritable spawning grounds for cutthroat trout.

During incoming and outgoing tides, many cuts will hang out in or near beach formations, such as points, big rocks, logs, and kelp beds, giving them protection from the current, a suitable resting spot, and a good place to watch for a meal as the baitfish pass by.

Anglers will also want to keep an eye on the baitfish, as this means your cuts are close behind. When buying or tying flies, small baitfish patterns in sizes 6–10 with olive, black, gray, or other dark colors are recommended. And after finding the perfect baitfish pattern, you'll also want to try and act like one, twitching and jumping to convince a cut to bite.

Averaging about 10–12 inches, these wild trout abound—some reaching up to 20 inches or more. And when spring comes around, fishing steadily gets better. Sea-run cuts, resident silvers, and black mouth become more active all around the Sound. Aspiring anglers will want to get out there and practice up before summertime runs roll into the neighborhood.

For such a small peninsula, the options are huge. Three prime locations and four fantastic species—all under 15 minutes from most parts of West Seattle.

What:
Fly Fish

Where:
Lincoln Park, Lowman Beach, and more
www.emeraldwateranglers.com
For reservations, contact Dave McCoy at 206.545.2197

When:
Whenever you have the fever for fishing. Trips offered all year long. Summer months are the prime season, so schedule early as they fill up fast.

Price:
A half-day trip runs $265 for one or two persons (many people split it).

Full day-trips are $325.

All trips include snacks, drinks, flies, leader, tippet, gear, etc.

5 | Celebrate with the Argosy Christmas Ship

Hit the beach for holiday cheer each year as the Argosy Christmas ship visits West Seattle. The ship has been spreading the spirit of the season on the high seas for more than half a century now, and greeting it at the waterfont has become a neighborhood tradition.

At the shoreline, crowds gather around toasty bonfires and sip cocoa while awaiting the floating guest of honor.

At the shoreline, crowds gather around toasty bonfires and sip cocoa while awaiting the floating guest of honor. As she approaches, you can hear the sound of carols echo across the water, building louder and louder as she sails closer. When she arrives, the Christmas ship and her flotilla of parade boats are adorned with colorful lights. Festivity fills the winter air as Northwest-area choirs on deck belt out their favorite tunes, which are broadcast via loudspeaker to shore.

Nearly every holiday season the boat visits Lowman Beach, Alki Beach, and Don Armeni Park on Harbor Avenue at least once in December. Grab a *West Seattle Herald* for location and date listings or visit the Argosy website, as the schedule varies each year.

One thing does remain constant year after year. You can count on the weather to be chilly and often downright cold. So bundle up, bring a thermos full of your favorite steaming beverage, and sing along with the heartwarming holiday tunes to make your cheeks rosy and heat you up from the inside out.

And if you'd rather catch a glimpse of West Seattle's beaches from the water side, embark on the holiday ships themselves for an entire evening of Yuletide fun. Argosy sells tickets for each ship in the parade.

The *Spirit of Seattle*, dubbed the "official" Christmas ship, is the leader of the pack with a myriad of decorated parade boats that follow. If you're feeling like shaking off a little humbug, splurge for the Royal Argosy package, complete with a freshly prepared three-course meal. Most ships in the fleet include a white-bearded, red suit-wearing special guest and onboard activities for the kids.

However you participate, the event is definitely more memorable than the typical holiday party. Best of all, you get to toast the season while becoming part of a Westside holiday tradition. So, join the joyful jaunt of the Argosy Christmas ship. And don't forget your mittens.

What:
Argosy Christmas Ship

Where:
West Seattle Beaches (Lowman, Alki, and Don Armeni Park)
www.argosycruises.com
206.623.1445

When:
Early to mid-December between 7and 10 pm (check as schedule changes each year)

Price:
Free from the beach. Prices vary for the onboard event; call for details.

6 | Disc Golf at Lakewood Park

It's called golf but requires no clubs. Nor are there huge fees or funny plaid pants. You do need a little time, however, and enough energy to scoot around from target to target.

We're talking about a round of disc golf at Lakewood County Park.

And if ten-time World Champion Ralph Williamson is there, he'll give you a tip or two. The retired Boeing engineer has been disc golfing for nearly three decades and loves to turn new people on to the sport.

Played with Frisbees, disc golf is similar to ball golf. According to Williamson, disc golf is the "real golf."

The two sports are closely related in structure. The object of both games is to get the ball or disc into the basket in as few strokes as possible. They even use the same terminology, like par, birdie, ace (for a hole in one), bogie (for one over par), and double bogie.

Disc golfers also yell out the same four-letter word if their flying disc is about to hit someone: "Fore!"

The sport also features bunkers, water traps, lake hazards, and out of bounds (which costs you a stroke penalty). The fairways are approximately one-third the length of a ball golf course, so they are usually just three pars, rather than golf's typical four and five pars.

> "Everyone should try this sport— it's good exercise, keeps you loose, and hones your hand-eye coordination."
>
> Ralph Williamson
> disc golf champion

"The sport exploded, like a mushroom cloud in late '60s, early '70s," recalls Williamson.

Williamson's specialty started in freestyle. He and his Frisbee-tossing buddies even did half-time shows for the Super Sonics in the old Seattle Coliseum. He eventually gravitated to disc golf and helped to develop the sport.

"Disc golf didn't start out with

courses, so we chose other things to make targets such as trees, lamp-posts, fire hydrants, garbage cans, you name it," explains Williamson.

The sport's next evolution was when the disc golf association invented a target made with a metal basket, a frame, and chains. When the disc hits, the chains absorb the energy, the disc falls into basket, and you've made your put!

Nowadays, disc golf courses, such as the one at Lakewood, offer full marked targets free of charge for the public to enjoy. The 35-acre course located near Evergreen High School began in 1987 when the County Parks Department bought the first nine holes and a group of devout players bought the second nine.

Williamson offers clinics on how to play the sport now and then, but if you go to Lakewood often enough, you'll eventually run into him. And while the equipment required is minimal, you do need to BYOD (bring your own discs).

"Everyone should try this sport—it's good exercise, keeps you loose, and hones your hand-eye coordination," encourages Williamson.

So take it from an expert. And get your golf game on—without all the trappings.

What:
Disc Golf

Where:
Lakewood County Park
11000 10th Ave. SW
White Center
www.odsa.com

Rules:
See rules at:
www.pdga.com

When:
Year-round

Price:
Free; BYOD (bring your own discs)

7 | Take the West Seattle Garden Tour

Travel to a land filled with Japanese maples. Sit in the shade of a Mediterranean fan palm. Or imagine sipping a cup of tea in an estate-like English garden—all without ever leaving West Seattle.

Welcome to the West Seattle Garden Tour—an annual event each summer in July made for green thumbs and novices alike.

> *"A lot of people take away a sense that 'hey, I can do that myself!'"*
>
> Marsha Kremen
> tour volunteer

Run by local volunteers, tour organization is a year-long process of surveying and selecting the perfect variety of gardens to showcase West Seattle's most diverse and innovative outdoor ideas. Garden "tourists" of all ages and skill levels come from around Puget Sound to see this oasis of intriguing and inspiring gardens.

"We get folks from Bellevue, Renton, Kent, Shoreline, Bainbridge, and beyond," remarks volunteer Marsha Kremen. "We also encourage novices to come. There is no better environment for people to learn than from the gathering of knowledgeable gardeners that are always here."

And this is no small crowd.

"We usually expect upwards of 700 attendees," says Kremen. "One year we walked almost 900 people through the gardens."

Besides providing a fun way to spend a summer day, the Garden Tour sparks ideas and makes the rather daunting task of building a great garden more approachable.

"A lot of people take away a sense that 'hey, I can do that myself,'" explains Kremen. "We have a broad cross-section of gardens that people can identify with, which gives them inspiration, design, and plant ideas for their own gardens."

A selection of unique sites are chosen for the tour each year. Gardens of various sizes, ages, and special themes are included—each one created to showcase the owners' personal vision and style. So keep your eyes out for what's blooming this year and contact the Garden Tour committee to find out the details.

And while you're touring, you'll be giving back to the community as well. Begun in 1995 as a fundraising event for ArtsWest Theatre, the West Seattle Garden Tour has evolved into an annual fundraising event for a variety of horticultural and educational organizations in West Seattle and its surrounds.

What:
Garden Tour

Where:
Neighborhood gardens
(changes each year)
www.westseattlegardentour.org
206.938.0963

When:
Usually third Sunday in July
(call or check website for date)

Price:
Tour tickets $15

8 | Dive into Colman Pool

Looking for a cool, watery oasis to escape the summer heat? How about snapping out a few laps after a steamy day at the office? Or maybe you'd simply like to see one of the best views in Seattle.

There's a swimming hole right here in West Seattle that's just as scenic as a dip the Sound but considerably warmer.

Dive into Colman Pool.

A strikingly unique place to splash around, the huge, heated pool contains 450,000 gallons of saltwater pulled straight from Puget Sound and maintained at a comfortable 82 degrees F.

Whether you're 7 or 77, this 50-meter mecca for water sports is the perfect place to work out or play all summer long. From Memorial Day to Labor Day (and then some), Colman offers pool parties, recreational public swims, fun family swims, invigorating lap swims (with fast, medium, and easy lane options), coached masters workouts, Hydro-Fit water exercise classes with resistance equipment, kickboards, water noodles, high and low dives, and a wild ride on the new corkscrew slide.

> **"Colman Pool is one of Seattle's best kept secrets."**
>
> Mark Sears
> second-generation pool operator

Because Colman Pool is located on the "point" at Lincoln Park, getting there is half the fun. If you live close, try biking. Or bring your trail shoes and walk through the park, picnicking along the way. If it's your first time, make a day of it.

"Colman is one of Seattle's best kept secrets," says second-generation pool operator Mark Sears. "Every day I hear people say 'this is great and I didn't even know it was here.' But it's been here for quite some time."

The pool is also soaked in history. Just step inside and you'll notice the historical "Youth and Freedom" mural depicting the Colman legacy. The piece was painted by renowned muralist Ernest Norling (who also did an oil painting selected to hang in the White House).

"Every image in the mural has something to do with the Colman family and this community," says Sears. The Colmans were paramount in starting the Fauntleroy Church and YMCA. "And these were during the times when you had to take a boat to get to West Seattle," he adds.

Ken Colman built the pool and donated it to the city as a memorial to his father Lawrence.

"I knew Ken Colman and his intention was to create an active outlet for youth," explains Sears. "He saw what he could do with this place—he designed, engineered, and built it, then handed it to the city as a gift. It's our responsibility to continue his vision."

Striving to do just that, Sears is only the second operator in the pool's history. The first operator was his dad Norman, who was hired by Ken Colman in 1941. Before starting at Colman Pool, Norman Sears ran Alki's bathing suit rentals and steam laundry services. He held the coveted steam engineer's license that was necessary to run the boilers for the new heated pool.

A historic landmark. An amazing exercise venue. And the scenery? Second to none. Locals say the only problem with Colman is that summer's too short. But West Seattleites will have to take that one up with Mother Nature.

What:
Colman Pool

Where:
The "point" at Lincoln Park
8603 Fauntleroy Way SW
www.cityofseattle.net/parks
206.684.7494

When:
Generally, the pool is open from Memorial Day to Labor Day; call for dates

Price:
Call for prices

9 | SCUBA Dive Elliott Bay

Ever noticed the floating red flags and mysterious seal-like creatures bobbing around in the waves off West Seattle? Slap on some fins, take a few backward steps from Alki Beach, and you'll find that a whole new underwater world awaits you.

> *"I've seen these octopi hundreds of times, but every time it's amazing."*
>
> Steve Steunenberg
> diver

"Elliott Bay is 95 percent devoid of currents, making it the premier dive spot in Puget Sound in terms of safety and ease for beginners," says diver Steve Steunenberg. As a result, local dive shop Deep Fathom (as well as other shops from all over the city) offers classes here, and numerous dive clubs often frequent the Westside's ideal beginner waters.

But calm water security is not the only attraction.

Elliott Bay is also home to some of the most magnificent sea creatures on the planet. Take for example the Pacific giant octopus—a species indigenous to the Northwest. Ranging in size from 8 to 10 feet, this nocturnal flurry of flowing tentacles sneaks out of its den to wow night divers, tempting them back into the water time and time again. "I've seen these octopi hundreds of times," explains Steunenberg. "But every time it's amazing."

The area is also habitat for wolf eels, large but approachable ling cod, sculpin, cabezon, gunnels, and a wide variety of rockfish including red snapper.

To learn more about these mystical creatures of the deep, venture to the Seattle Aquarium where Northwest fish and marine life thrive. During spring and summer months, you can take the Elliott Bay Water Taxi to the aquarium. The rest of the year, visit by bike, car, or bus, or see it online at www.seattleaquarium.org. Once your study session is done, you can find the various marine animals and fish on your own in the wild—which is all the more fun.

Like an underwater treasure hunt, the Sound is full of amazing wildlife gems you might never see otherwise. And sure, snorkeling can give you a feel for what lies below. But SCUBA diving lets you pretend, if only for a short time, that you too belong beneath the surface, swimming with these creatures.

For SCUBA divers who are already certified, find out more in-depth information on West Seattle dives at www.nwdivenews.com.

Or, if you've never tried to SCUBA dive and you're ready to take the plunge, you can sign up to be certified through most Seattle dive shops —just make sure to request West Seattle classes. Deep Fathom offers certification classes from instructors Sean Rapson and Craig Gillespie. In fact, Gillespie was recently awarded the highest number of student certifications in the history of Professional Association of Diving Instructors (PADI). For more info on Gillespie himself, visit his site at www.seattlescuba.com.

So grab your wetsuits and fins, and get ready to dive in. The octopi are waiting!

What:
SCUBA Dive

Where:
Deep Fathom Dive Supply
2645 Harbor Ave. SW
Seattle WA 98126
www.deepfathom.com
206.938.7784

For a listing of other Seattle dive shops:
www.scubanorthwest.com

When:
24/7 if you're advanced; beginners call for class times.

Price:
Prices vary; please call or check web for details.

10 | Picnic in the Park

A picnic in the park may sound like something out of Mayberry, but with West Seattle's plentiful greenspace, wildlife, and enchanting views, this traditional pastime makes for primetime fun.

Grab your cooler or picnic basket, a red and white checkered blanket, and some tasty treats, and you're all set. In fact, preparing your picnic meal is easier than ever before.

Unless you yearn for the taste of homemade potato salad and self-stacked sandwiches, the handful of gourmet West Seattle delis make picnic-packing a low-maintenance activity. Drop by Husky Deli in the junction, Metropolitan Market on Admiral, or PCC for everything from traditional baked beans to sushi—pre-made and packed for transport.

Besides choosing what delicacies to bring for your mobile feast, pre-planning your picnic ambience is a must. Do you want a dreamy sunset to set the mood for two or would you rather bring the extended fam, dogs, and Frisbees? Here are a few ideas to put you in picnic mode.

Romantic sunset picnic at Hamilton Viewpoint
If you're sweet on city views, sunsets, and your significant other, Hamilton Viewpoint will make you swoon. Atop the bluff in North Admiral, enjoy the scenic picture painted by the boats of Elliott Bay, night-lit skyscrapers, and the pinkish-purple backdrop of the Cascades.

You can impress your partner with a little Westside history, too. In 1957 Hamilton Viewpoint was named to honor Rupert Lehn Hamilton in recognition of his efforts to promote parks and viewpoints in West Seattle while he was editor and publisher of the *West Seattle Herald.*

Wander the wooded trails and cross the gurgling creek in the canopy of a mini old-growth forest.

Picnic with your pooch at Westcrest
If your idea of picnicking also includes tennis balls and doggie biscuits, bring your four-legged friend to Westcrest Park. Enjoy your meal while taking in the

panoramic view of the city skyline in the park proper. Then let your pooch go burn off those dog treats in the off-leash area.

Extended family extravaganza at Me-Kwa-Mooks
Me-Kwa-Mooks Natural Area is an intimate Puget Sound locale with views of Blake Island and the Olympic Mountains. This spot offers both grassy open space and beachcombing across the street. Sprawl out on the lawn with the entire family and set up the croquet set or tiptoe through the tide pools (actually, the critters prefer you walk around them rather than right through their watery dwellings).

Picnic among the pine trees at Schmitz

Prefer the shade of a mighty cedar tree for your picnic? Visit Schmitz Preserve Park, where you can wander the wooded trails and cross the gurgling creek in the canopy of a mini old-growth forest.

Named after Ferdinand Schmitz, a German immigrant living in West Seattle, the park is a result of Schmitz's concern for Washington's rapidly decreasing forests. Thanks to his efforts, we can still share the awe of old-growth trees while nibbling on sandwiches today.

What:
Picnic in the Park

Where:
Hamilton Viewpoint
1531 California Ave. SW
206.684.4075

Westcrest Park
9000 8th Ave. SW
www.cityofseattle.net
206.684.4075

Me-Kwa-Mooks
4100 Aikins Ave SW
www.cityofseattle.net
206.684.4075

Schmitz Preserve Park
5551 SW Admiral Way
www.schmitzpark.org
206.684.4075

When:
Year-round (weather permitting)

Price:
The view is free, the food'll cost ya.

11 | Storm Watch at Seattle's Best Spots

Ask people in this city what they know about West Seattle and most will say they've been to Alki Beach—in the summer. But many have yet to discover that there's something special here during winter months, too: spectacular storm watching.

> West Seattle is a prime spot to watch squalls, whitecaps, and windstorms as they come in from all directions.

West Seattle is a prime spot to watch squalls, whitecaps, and windstorms as they come from all directions. While some brave the storm outside, others choose to stay dry and protected in their cars. It's safe as long as you stay clear of big trees and falling branches. And the best thing about this beach activity is that it requires zero SPF. You might, however, want to bring an umbrella meant for rain rather than sun and a beach bag full of warm clothes and cocoa.

Here are a few rather cold hotspots to catch the action.

Constellation Park
Where Alki Avenue turns into Beach Drive (near the lighthouse) you will find excellent views for both outdoor and car-style storm watching. And in the odd chance that the sky clears, you can look up and stargaze, too. As the park name states, it's definitely appropriate.

Alki Beach
Brave the beach. Park, and watch in your car. Or, sit inside a cozy restaurant. Pegasus Pizza, Dukes, Pepperdock, and upstairs at Spuds offer great indoor viewing. And if you prefer a slightly more serene sea but bigger views, go around the corner to Salty's for giant picture windows.

The point at Lincoln Park
Just in front of Colman Pool is the point at Lincoln Park where you can

catch the storms from both sides. If it's windy, hold on to your hats because this area is very exposed to the elements. Parking is available at the lots along Fauntleroy Way or at the north end of the park near Lowman Beach.

Sunset Avenue in North Admiral
This one is a bit tough for parking but has some of the best long-range views from atop the weatherworn cliff.

What:
Storm Watch

Where:
Constellation Park
Alki Beach
Lincoln Park
Sunset Ave. in North Admiral
www.cityofseattle.net/parks

When:
October–April; watch your
local weather forecast

Price:
Free of charge from
Mother Nature

12 | Go Geocaching

Think you know your way around West Seattle? Challenge yourself to find new routes through the neighborhood with an outdoor game that befuddles even the savviest native. Introducing geocaching.

Started in Portland, Oregon, during the spring of 2000 and quickly spreading all the way up to West Seattle, geocaching is a modern-day treasure hunt.

Using Global Positioning System (GPS) receivers to move you from one set of coordinates to another, you follow a course that eventually lands you in a final cache location where other geocachers have previously hidden prizes for your discovery.

It's a great way to get outside for some exercise and get your mind working as well.

So, how do you instigate this venture? First, go to www.geocaching. com. Once you have chosen your West Seattle cache, enter the location's coordinates into your GPS receiver to find out how far away and in what direction the cache lies—two dozen satellites in low Earth orbit can't steer you wrong.

You proceed from point to point with simple activities followed by equations such as counting the bolts on a bench and multiplying that number by five (see website for specific clues).

And the journey is just as fun as finding the hidden cache. You often need to navigate obstacles such as cliffs, water, or impassable structures. Some choose to conquer their cache on foot, by bike, or even via kayak.

Arrive at it how you wish, but once you finally catch on to the cache and complete the course, make sure you've remembered to bring a prize. Following the take-a-prize-give-a-prize philosophy, you are allowed to grab the prize you find waiting, but you must replace it with another for the next geocacher who happens upon the site.

> *The journey is just as fun as finding the hidden cache.*

What are some typical cache tchotskies? Depending on the size of the cache, you may find toys, trinkets, CDs, or even a nibble of food. You'll also find a log book where you can prove your feat and scribble notes for future cache visitors.

A great outdoor activity for any age, geocaching can be played by individual adventurers, families, and couples. And while the prizes aren't big, the reward of spending time outdoors with friends or family and challenging your brain in new ways is definitely worth the trek.

To try geocaching yourself, look up one of many West Seattle locations on the geocache website. Here are a couple favorites.

Schmitz Preserve Park
N 47° 34.510 W 122° 24.121 (WGS84)
UTM: 10T E 544972 N 5269257

Stroll under the canopy of old growth while hunting for your treasure—no bushwhacking necessary.

Alki Tour #2 Cache
N 47° 35.113 W 122° 22.110 (WGS84)
UTM: 10T E 547483 N 5270394

A 10- to 12-mile waterfront course perfect for geocaching by bike.

What:
Geocaching

Where:
Alki, Schmitz Park
and more
www.geocaching.com

When:
Year-round

Price:
Free; but you will need to borrow or buy a GPS receiver (they usually start around $100)

13 | Salmon Fish in Westside Waters

Nearly every summer, there's a buzz by the water. When the salmon are here, boats of all sizes speckle the shore. The pier is packed and fish are rising on the horizon. From the last of the pinks to the kings and silvers, they're swimming 'round the Sound, so catch one if you can.

> *Anglers at Seacrest Marina have been known to catch up to 36-pound king salmon off the pier.*

The options are numerous. Spin fish or fly fish. Boat it, wade it, or pier it. Seacrest Marina offers pier fishing and also rents aluminum Lunds with outboards by the hour. And many prefer to wade right in at area beaches.

If you're going for pinks, or humpies, they're here on odd-numbered years, so "appreciate" them when you can.

Silvers, or coho, also run until mid- or late October. These fish feature a white lower gum line and a dark bluish-green back and head. So load up on white and blue Buzz Bombs, spoons, herring, or darts, and get ready.

Kings, otherwise known as Chinook or blackmouth, are the largest salmon swimming in our waters. Kings spawn from September through mid-December. And if you're lucky enough to catch one, you'll know it's a king by its black lower gum line and 24- to 60-inch length (if it's less than 22 inches, you'll have to throw it back). Catch and release is also always an option, of course.

Anglers at Seacrest Marina have been known to catch up to 36-pound kings off the pier, and those who have ventured offshore have brought in 45-pounders from the east waterway in the past.

What do they use? Traditionalists swear by herring, and early adapters say that downriggers are the way to go. Many think it has to do with luck—after all, it's not called "fishing" for nothing.

If you don't already have a fishing license, Seacrest sells 2-day and season saltwater permits. At press time, the catch limit on salmon was two per angler. As with anything, know your limit and double-check the rules before you go.

You can read up on the "regs" in the catch book or on the Washington State Fish and Wildlife website www.wa.gov/wdfw.

And do check it out, because rules change. One thing that's for sure, all hooks must be barbless or the Fish and Game Department will issue you a ticket. So make sure you pinch your hooks down and you won't get pinched yourself.

Never salmon fished in West Seattle before? Don't let regulars and old-timers intimidate you. The fish don't care. Men, women, and kids of all ages can cast with high hopes and have fun just being out there on the water.

What:
Salmon Fish

Where:
From Seacrest Marina
(and by boat)
1660 Harbor Ave SW
206.938.0975

When:
Late Summer through
October

Price:
Call Seacrest for bait,
licenses, and boat rental
prices

RECREATION

14 | *Go Birdwatching*

Many birders travel far to see their feathered friends. In fact, it's not uncommon for hardcore birdwatchers to venture to exotic locales just to find them. But local fans of the winged species will be happy to know that there's some great birdwatching (and listening) close to home.

West Seattle's plethora of parks creates an ideal habitat for many species. From Fauntleroy Park on Barton to Schmitz and Lincoln, if you take the time to look and listen, you're sure to discover many a bird and a new song or two.

> *"I once saw an eagle trying to pirate a fish from an osprey at Lincoln Park."*
>
> Linda Gresky
> Seattle Audubon Society

What are you are likely to see? The small, brown Bewick's wren for one, as well as little green Anna's hummingbirds and golden-crowned kinglets.

"Small birds with a whitish chest, olive back, and gold markings on the head, golden-crowned kinglets look like they're wearing little crowns," says Linda Gresky, a volunteer for the Seattle Audubon Society and Fauntleroy Watershed Council.

But there's more than just these three. Head toward the water to witness ducks and an array of birds of prey. It's not uncommon to see buffleheads (ducks with white markings resembling small, white hats), harlequin ducks (with spectacular markings and white slashes across the head and shoulders), and the infamous surf scoter with a bill so brilliant orange you'd think you were spotting him in the tropics.

Bald eagles and osprey also fit the bill. "Because they are such great fishers, the osprey is also known as the sea hawk," explains Gresky. "In fact, I once saw an eagle trying to pirate a fish from an osprey at Lincoln Park."

Entertainment for all seasons, birding is enjoyable for people of every age.

"Birdwatching is almost like a scavenger hunt to kids," explains Gresky. "It's a great way to let them explore, check their findings against the field guide, and feel like they've found something special."

For beginning birders, Gresky has helpful advice. "The birds may be difficult to identify at first, but if you have patience and stick to it, you'll get it," she smiles. "And when you do, it's exciting."

Likening birdwatching to a release that brings one back to center, Gresky reflects, "It is one of most peaceful experiences there is. Nowhere else are you more in the moment than out there in nature birdwatching."

One of the best ways to get into birding is with a field trip. Local group trips offer the expertise of master birders, a chance to meet others with similar interests in nature, and a fun yet educational excuse to get outside. Visit the Seattle Audubon Society website for more info at www.seattleaudubon.org.

You'll want to bring field glasses or binoculars, a Northwest bird identification book (*Birds of Seattle & Puget Sound* recommended), and a notepad for sketching.

Whether they are surfing the waves, perched in a tree, or soaring high above, birds from the common loon to a yellow-bellied sapsucker make their homes in West Seattle. Next time you're out and about, look out and up for the feathered phenoms of the neighborhood.

What:
Bird Watching

Where:
West Seattle's Parks such as Fauntleroy, Lincoln, and Schmitz
www.cityofseattle.net/parks

When:
Year-round

Price:
Free; BYOB (bring your own binocs)

15 | Stargaze at Constellation Park

After a busy day at the office or a weekend of running errands, nothing's nicer than taking a moment to sit back, look up, and get lost in the glorious night sky at Constellation Park. Pick a clear evening, and you'll be amazed at what you might find.

Where Alki Avenue meets Beach Drive, just southeast of the lighthouse, Constellation Park awaits gazers of stars, planets, and the moon. A long stretch of beach complemented by a sidewalk complete with inset models of constellations, this spot is not only a good place to watch the sky but also has built-in maps to help guide you.

When you go stargazing, travel to the park after dark and bring a headlamp or flashlight to view the constellation maps on the sidewalk below (red LED lights are recommended to retain your best "night vision"). While viewing the model, memorize the shape and pattern of the stars then turn off your light source and wait for your eyes to adjust to the dark. Peer skyward and see what you can find.

Some common constellations to look for in West Seattle's sky are the Big Dipper, Cassiopeia, Orion, Sagittarius, and Leo. Need a few tips? First, search for the brightest stars in the night sky. Once you've spotted an especially bright star, such as Polaris (or the North Star), "connect the dots" to reveal entire constellations like the Big Dipper. Note that the "zenith" is the highest point in the sky (directly overhead), and the horizon is the line where the sky appears to touch the earth.

> This spot is not only a good place to watch the night sky but also has built-in maps to help guide you.

When searching for planets, you'll probably have to get up at the crack of dawn to find the bright, colorful bodies shining in the morning sky.

Some planets to keep your eye out for are:

• Mercury, the winged messenger that lives closest to the Sun

- Venus, named after the goddess of love and beauty because it was the brightest planet known to the ancients

- Mars, the bringer of war, also known as the Red Planet

- Jupiter, the fifth planet from the Sun—more than twice the size of all the other planets combined

- Saturn, the sixth planet from the Sun, the second largest in our solar system, and the origin of the English word "Saturday"

Stargazing is a fun solo activity, but it's also great in a group. For monthly star parties and more information, contact the Seattle Astronomic Society at www.seattleastro.org or the Pacific Science Center at www.pacsci.org.

What:
Stargazing

Where:
Constellation Park
(where Alki Ave meets
Beach Dr just south of
the lighthouse)
www.cityofseattle.
net/parks/parkspaces/
richeyviewpoint.htm
206.684.4075

When:
Year-round whenever
skies are clear

Price:
Free

16 | Unleash at WestCrest Dog Park

Walk up over the grassy hill and you'll witness a panoramic view of the city skyline. Take a few steps further and you'll see unusual movements between the trees and above the low-lying brush. They're tails—tons of them—wagging with pure joy. And they belong to local pups who have found a place to call their own: WestCrest Dog Park.

> **"If he [Corey] knows he's going to the dog park he starts levitating —bouncing up and down!"**
>
> Barbara Brown
> dog owner

Featuring a doggie drinking fountain, more than four acres of grass, open spaces and paths for the pooches, plus benches, chairs, sheltered shade, and restrooms for the owners, this dog park is one of Seattle's nine off-leash areas where dogs are free to run, roll over, and make new friends.

On any given day, you're bound to bump into everything from a bunch of baying basset hounds and speedy little Jack Russells to happy-go-lucky Labs and mutts a-plenty.

Corey, a lucky yellow Lab, comes to WestCrest two or three times per week.

"He's a perpetual-motion machine," smiles owner Barbara Brown of Morgan Junction. "If he knows he's going to the dog park he starts levitating—bouncing up and down!"

So does Corey's behavior mean that WestCrest is a good dog park? According to him, yes. And owners seem to enjoy it, too.

"There is room to move here," says Brown. "It's big, and the dogs aren't piled up on top of each other like they are at other dog parks."

But off-leash areas aren't just a bonus for the dogs and owners. They are also great for folks who aren't big fans of the four-legged ones.

"It keeps dogs in an enclosed area so they can enjoy themselves without bothering kids and people who don't want to be close to them," Brown explains.

So whether you have two legs or four, come see what's making tails wag at WestCrest.

Note to Dogs (please have owners read):
- To come and play in off-leash areas, you need to be licensed and vaccinated.
- If you wear a pinch or choke collar, ask your owner to remove it when you come into off-leash areas.
- If you're a puppy younger than four months or a female in heat, you are not allowed in off-leash areas.

Note to Dog Owners:
- You are liable for damage or injury inflicted by your dog and must be in control of your dog(s) at all times. Unattended dogs are not allowed.
- You must muzzle dogs that exhibit dangerous or aggressive behavior; biting, fighting, and excessive barking are not allowed.
- You must leash your dog when it is outside the off-leash area; you must carry a leash for each dog while you are inside the off-leash area.
- You must clean up after your dog(s) and deposit waste in the containers at the site, and you must visibly carry scoop equipment.
- You must closely supervise young children and only bring food into off-leash areas at your own risk.

Follow these simple and reasonable rules, and there's no end to the fun your furry friends can have.

What:
Dog Park

Where:
WestCrest Park
9000 8th Ave SW
www.ci.seattle.wa.us/
parks/parkspaces/
YoDogs.htm
206.684.4075

When:
Park hours are
4 am–11:30 pm

Price:
Free

17 | Play in the Snow

Whenever newscasters report the possibility of snow in Seattle, schoolkids begin to pray that when they awake the following day, their worlds will have magically turned fluffy and white—one peacefully falling flake at a time.

Adults, however, have mixed feelings about the chilly, crystalline change of pace. When snow hits the Westside, they tend to either dig it or dread it. On the one hand, it can make for horrendous driving and foul up work routines. But on the other, this cool change may just be a good thing.

Stumped by a snowfall? Since it's rare to see snow in these parts at all today, the best approach may be to take the time to frolic, go with the flow, and play in the snow. Try a few of these activities:

Get out of the car and enjoy the outdoors. Hop off the bus and call it a snow day. Take in the insulated silence of your snow-blanketed neighborhood. Forget about email piling up for a day and throw on your mittens to make snow angels instead. Bring the kids on a walk through the winter wonderland, marveling at how different the world looks in only one glorious hue. Or, simply be a kid yourself. Call your friends within walking distance and meet up for winter fun.

If building snowmen (and snow-women) is your thing, head to Fairmount Park for a field full of white stuff and plenty of elbow room. The elevation is high enough to keep snow when it's here, and the park's flat surroundings make for fairly good driving conditions and easy access.

When the snow hits, crowds gather atop Charlestown to watch kids and crazy grown-ups bomb down the hill in a fast-paced, snow-filled frenzy.

For snowball fights, Lincoln Park is the place to be—plenty of trees to hide behind and wide open fields to roll and stockpile your ammo. Hamilton Viewpoint and Camp Long provide similar but higher-elevation options (hence more lasting snow). So, if you can get there, go!

And if you want to take advantage of West Seattle's serious hills, go sledding, tubing, or tobogganing down the steepest street on the Westside: Charlestown. Following a truly exciting neighborhood tradition, crowds gather atop Charlestown when the snow hits to watch kids and crazy grown-ups bomb down the hill in a fast-paced, snow-filled frenzy.

Next time you feel a chill in the air and the flakes begin to float down around you, do not fret. Consider it Mother Nature's permission to play hooky—from school, from work, and from the usual way you view your surroundings.

What:
Play in the snow

Where:
West Seattle Parks
and more (the higher
elevation the better)
www.cityofseattle.
net/parks

When:
You'll know when you
see snow

Price:
Free; BYOM (bring
your own mittens)

18 | *Rockclimb at Allstar*

Bring your outdoor enthusiasm inside and scale the sportrock indoor climbing wall at Allstar Fitness. Beneath the giant glass atrium, the "tower" offers West Seattleites a chance to develop and hone climbing skills—under cover.

And while some climbers prefer the privacy of scaling the tower's back side, others enjoy being a spider-like spectacle, as the sportrock is perfectly situated for spectators in the lobby entrance to the club.

The tower is Allstar's icon, and the only public indoor sportrock of its kind between South Seattle and Tacoma.

"West Seattle is such an incredible place for outdoor enthusiasts, with kayaking, cycling, and more," says climbing director Dylan Johnson. "It's only fitting that there's a rock wall here for all the mountain-minded people who live in the area."

> *"It's only fitting that there's a rock wall here for all the mountain-minded people who live in the area."*
>
> Dylan Johnson
> Allstar climbing director

Johnson's been climbing for as long as he can remember.

"My dad was a climber," he reflects. "So I was exposed to the mountains before I could walk and have been active in the climbing community since age 12."

Like Johnson, local climbers are happy to have a place to work out so close to home. And beginners keep on coming to take the plunge...or the ascent rather. Novices need not worry. This tower is truly first-timer-friendly.

"This rock caters to beginners," explains Johnson. "A lot of people come into the sport intimidated at first, so here we start with the fundamentals, teach them everything they need to know, and let people really get good at the basics before letting them loose to climb some cliff in the Cascades."

Allstar offers the following courses:

• Juniors Program, a month-long class designed to provide a safe and fun environment for children to develop basic rock-climbing skills

• Rock 101, teaching the basics in a one-time, 2-hour class

• Pro-Belay, with expert supervision for those who need to hire a belayer

• Bouldering Cardio, an exciting 30-minute warm-up, climb, and cool-down class

• Sessions, instructor-led climbing workouts on Thursday nights

• Group Climbs, available for private parties, special events, and groups up to 12

According to Johnson, climbing is a great way to develop trust in yourself and your partners. And, as a group activity, it's a great team-building exercise as well as a healthy way for friends to get together and have a good time.

What:
Indoor Sportrock

Where:
Allstar Fitness
2629 SW Andover St.
www.allstarfitness.com
206.932.9999 ext. 7390

When:
Monday–Friday 5 am–11 pm
Saturday & Sunday 8 am–8 pm

Price:
Visit the website for member & non-member rates

"We recommend trying rock climbing for anyone who has never done it before, especially kids—they love it," encourages Johnson.

And experienced climbers will be glad to know that this rock also offers rotating routes featuring everything from a 5.6 to a 5.11 plus. Now that is a plus.

Thanks to all these options—and Allstar's weatherproof roof—you can rock on in all seasons.

19 | Kite Surf in Westside Wind

Head down to the east end of Alki, and you may see a colorful kite whip wildly in the wind. Every few seconds, there's a splash below as its operator lands a wave. If the north wind is blowing, chances are wetsuit-wearing water-nuts are out there kite surfing.

"I love to jump," beams West Seattle kite surfer Tom Dawson. "It feels like flying."

A relatively new water sport that relies on the mighty power of wind, the activity combines board-riding with kite-flying. Some call it sailing, others call it surfing. But true kite boarders searching for a suitable term often refer to their hallowed hobby as "flying."

So what exactly is kite surfing? According to Dawson, kite surfing is "like low-level gliding, almost like swinging from a rope."

But it's much more technical than that sounds. And if you dare to get air, you've got to know the ropes first. Most enthusiasts start by getting to know the kites.

There are many types of kites to choose from, but the majority of kite surfers use what is called a marine wing. Developed by Frenchman Bruno Legaignoux, the unit features an inflated leading edge and five struts to give it shape.

These kites are maneuvered in a 3D window, allowing for better control and more power. That's why you see surfers weighing 200 pounds and more catch huge air, often 10 feet or better. But with all that power, you've got to log a lot of practice hours to safely get the hang of the proper technique.

"If you're gentle with the kite, it is gentle with you," advises Dawson. "But if you're aggressive with the kite, it will end up flying you around."

He compares the kite to having a big dog at the end of a leash.

So where does one begin?

> ## "It feels like flying."
>
> Tom Dawson
> kite surfer

According to Dawson, you must first learn how to operate a kite on land with a "trainer kite." Lessons are offered in other parts of Seattle, but once they advance, kite surfers dig Alki.

"I love Alki. It's a real crowd pleaser," says Dawson. "There's a real beach scene, more than any other area in Seattle."

But with considerable boat and beach traffic, boarders must know what they're doing and be able to control themselves in tight situations. So take your time. Learn to fly right. And when you're really ready, consider Alki as the prize.

'Cause if the wind is kicking, there's no place a kite surfer would rather be.

"I always say, never leave wind to find wind," nods Dawson. "If it's windy in West Seattle, that's where I'll be."

What:
Kite Surf

Where:
Off Alki Beach

When:
Year-round for hardcore surfers, summertime for most

Prices:
(for Lessons & Gear)
www.gokiting.com
www.urbansurf.com
www.wileyski.com

20 | Scoot Along on a Segway

Straight out of a scene on "The Jetsons" comes West Seattle's high-tech way to cruise the strip: the Segway Human Transporter.

Originally referred to as the "IT," this revolutionary, self-balancing vehicle's code name changed to Ginger before it finally hit the streets as the official Segway that you see cruising the hood today.

> *"It feels like you're gliding on air."*
>
> Craig Vinton
> rental entrepreneur

Segways are small, collapsible for travel, and environmentally friendly. In fact, these runabouts are so quiet that the manufacturers had to re-engineer them to increase the engine noise so pedestrians could hear them coming.

"It feels like you're gliding on air," smiles Segway rental entrepreneur Craig Vinton.

Vinton has owned West Seattle's AllStar Entertainment since 1981. The company is not only the first in the area to pioneer Segway rentals but has also graced the city with crazy corporate party hits such as Psuedo-Sumo wrestling, the Velcro Wall, GyroTrons, and gladiator jousts.

"Our company is all about offering the latest in fun ideas," says Vinton. "We're always dreaming up new things, and renting the Segway was one of them."

AllStar was chosen for the Segway ambassador program to help bring exposure to the vehicle.

"We had to go to the manufacturers in New Hampshire for training and were lucky to offer them before anybody else," nods Vinton.

AllStar offers six vehicles, so you can ride with your friends or family, or keep it simple and go solo.

The Segways can be rented by the hour to scoot around the neighborhood, or they can be rented for corporate parties, parades, trade shows, and other events. Interested drivers just have to call to schedule a start time at the Fauntleroy location then run through the instructional training and safety course before letting loose on the road.

Legal and approved for sidewalk traffic in 35 states, Segways can be driven on Alki's retail sidewalk and in the street (just not on the bike lane, please). And they zip along at about 13 miles per hour. But are they safe?

"You literally can't fall off them. In fact, I have a lot of older clients who can't walk down to the beach and choose to rent these instead," continues Vinton. "Segways are a great way to get around and maneuver really well."

According to Vinton, they also attract a lot of attention, which renters seem to revel in.

"People are really curious and tend to stare at you as you drive by. It's fun."

There are some limitations, however. Segways can't hop high curbs, and they run on batteries that limit you to 18 miles of travel.

"So we have a route system and suggested places to plug in if the need arises," assures Vinton.

If you're bored with biking or 'blading it down the beach, check out the scene a new way—via Segway. Just don't be surprised if you pass Rosie the Robot as you scoot along.

What:
Scoot Along on a Segway

Where:
AllStar Entertainment
4350 SW Frontenac
www.allstar-fun.com
206.919.3023

When:
Year-round, nice weather's a plus

Price:
Call for rates

21 | Go on a Walkabout

Want to find out what West Seattle's all about? Maybe it's time to go on a walkabout.

An Australian term referring to Aboriginal wanderings through the bush, a walkabout can be just as rewarding Out West as it is Down Under.

By taking the time to stroll the streets and trails of West Seattle, you see certain things you tend to miss when zooming along in your car. You talk to people you'd normally pass right on by. And you get to know the place better when you feel it beneath your feet.

With its varied terrain, West Seattle offers a wonderland for walkabouts.

Up for a flat but scenic beach stroll? Do the 3-mile Alki jaunt along Alki and Harbor Avenues from Starbucks to Salty's and back for a good 6-mile round trip.

Like a little bit of a challenge and some serious hills? Try the Alki-Admiral loop. Start at Alki Café, follow Alki Avenue east as it turns into Harbor Avenue, then hang a right on California and venture up the winding hill along the cliff, past Hamilton Viewpoint and up to Admiral Way. Once you hit Admiral, take a right and saunter back down the hill to the beach.

> *Get to know the place better simply by feeling it beneath your feet.*

Maybe you're in the market for more of a retail rambling? Get to know California Avenue like you never have before by doing the whole darn thing—north to south or south to north…and back! There are plenty of rest stops along the way where you can refuel. Coffee at Café Lladro. Ice Cream at Husky Deli. Bagels at Zatz. You can also window-shop or step inside the stores. Browse for new tunes at Easy Street. Or check out the latest housewares at Capers. Just don't buy too much or you'll have to forego the walkabout and bus it home.

Looking for more of a nature experience? Lincoln Park offers a series of tree-lined trails as well as beach walks. If a shorter walkabout is your style, Schmitz Park offers a shade-laden old-growth canopy under which to wander (which is Bill Nye the Science Guy's favorite Westside walkabout).

Whichever walkabout suits your style, you don't need much gear. Just a good pair of walking shoes and a healthy combination of patience, curiosity, and appreciation for two-legged travel.

What:
Walkabout

Where:
Alki, Admiral,
Lincoln Park and
California Ave

When:
Year-round

Price:
Free; BYOS (bring
your own shoes)

22 | Skim Board at Anchor Park

Ready to slip and slide on the Westside? Try skim boarding at Anchor Park on Alki.

"It's a lot like skateboarding, except you do it on the water," says skim boarder and Alki Bike and Board owner Stu Hennessey.

"Some people, especially lighter-weight riders, are able to kick along the water and skim like a skateboarder," explains Hennessey. "But most of us just throw down our boards, jump on, and ride."

> *"It's a lot like skateboarding, except you do it on the water."*
>
> Stu Hennessey
> skim boarder and
> Alki Bike & Board owner

Skim boards are thin, relatively flat, oval-shaped discs sized to fit their riders. The ratio is simple: the bigger the rider, the bigger the board.

A rider's timing must also be just right, as there's a fairly small window of ride time when the water depth, momentum, and beach slope are ideal.

"When the wave begins to subside, you throw the board down ahead of you and get a running start," describes Hennessey. "Then you jump onto the board and your momentum creates pressure that builds up below you, allowing you to skim along over the surface in shallow water."

Hence the name: skimming.

"It's best to skim in about an inch of water, sometimes even a little less," advises Hennessey. "But too little water, and you tend to bottom out or fall."

Skim boards are designed mainly for shallow water use, because the deeper the water, the less pressure there is to keep riders up. Some progressive riders, however, use the deeper water for tricks.

Traditional skim boards or "woodies" are meant for riding flat surfaces while the new "foamies" are better for deep-water tricks and riding surf. Again as in skateboarding, skim boarders are always trying to further the fun by adding grind rails and ramps into the mix. You'll see them down at the beach testing out their latest plastic ramps or drop-in slides.

"Rather than just relying on your own momentum, downhill runs also allow you to go faster and get more distance," smiles Hennessey. "We'll also use waves as a quarter pipe and do Ollies off the wake."

One of the best things about picking up the sport is that, besides your swim suit and bare feet, all you need is a board.

Where does one skim in West Seattle? Anchor Park on Alki is a prime location to ride. "I've gone to Canon Beach, Seaside, and Ocean Shores, which are great," reflects Hennessey. "But at low tide, you can't beat Alki."

So low tides are the ticket. Incoming tides are ideal for tricks. Outgoing tides give the best slope, longest shallows, and most helpful current running towards the surf. April and May are great months for low tides and June has a tradition of minus tides which is "primo" for riding.

Summer's a great time to pick up a fun, new sport. So grab a board, shuck off your shoes, and get skimming at one of the best spots in the West.

What:
Skim Board

Where:
Anchor Park on Alki
(AKA Duwamish Head)
Where Harbor Ave
turns into Alki Ave SW
www.skimonline.com/skim
spots/wash.htm

When:
Year-round, April–June for
best tides

Prices (for boards):
Alki Bike & Board
2606 California Ave SW
www.alkibikeandboard.com
206.938.3322

23 | Beach Cruise from Coastal

Slip on your "barely there" shoes and get ready to ride—So-Cal-style. Coastal Surf Boutique on Alki has Del Sol beach cruiser bicycles for hire, so you can saddle up for an hour or a day of laidback beach fun.

A surf, skate, and snow boutique and the first of its kind on Alki, Coastal opened its doors in '02 and now, in addition to offering the best selection of flip flops in town, it's bringing the fun of cruising back to the beach.

Whether you prefer two wheels or four, cruising has always been a part of Alki. And Coastal strives to keep that tradition alive, offering a fleet of stylish and new "Tradewinds" comfort cruisers with old-school style.

Inspired by San Diego's Mission Beach lifestyle, Coastal's co-founders claim that these cruisers and the beach belong together.

"All beach towns have cruisers for rent," smiles Coastal co-owner Sarah Steere. "You need to have beach cruisers here on the only true beach boardwalk in Seattle. It's the perfect thing to do."

"Cruising tops off a day full of activities," agrees co-owner Christy Metzger. "You can come down to the beach, grab something to eat, sip a smoothie, shop a bit, and now you can experience it all—by bike."

Both owners enjoy bike-commuting to work (especially on sunny summer days) and want to encourage the same fun and health-conscious attitude here on the beach.

> "Hopping on that beach cruiser and riding away gives you a real sense of freedom."
>
> Christy Metzger
> co-owner

"Hopping on that beach cruiser and riding away gives you a real sense of freedom," reflects Metzger. "It's an excuse to have fun and be young no matter what your age—a true escape."

With Alki's nearly 4 miles of paved trail (making it a cool 8-mile round trip for those who like the long haul), you can cover a comfortable amount of ground as you take in the sea breeze, Olympic Mountains, and downtown city views. The sounds of fading tunes provide a backdrop as convertibles cruise by street-side.

"It's a laidback activity that anyone can do," explains Steere. "And the cruisers are ultra-comfortable to ride because you sit upright and pedal with ease."

There's nothing quite like having the salt air and wind in your hair as you pedal away to your own rhythm, far from the hectic pace of life.

When summertime rolls, so can you—on a classic beach cruiser from Coastal.

What:
Beach Cruising

Where:
Coastal Surf Boutique
2532 Alki Ave SW
www.coastalseattle.com
206.933.5605

When:
Call for hours as rentals
are seasonal

Price:
Prices vary; call for
current rates

24 | Venture East to Seattle Chinese Garden

Want to take a quick trip to China and never leave West Seattle? Venture east up the hill from Delridge to the Seattle Chinese Garden.

Located on South Seattle Community College's North Campus, the Seattle Chinese Garden was conceived when Seattle became the sister city of Chongqing, China, in the '80s.

Step onto the raked gravel path, and you'll step into a beautifully intriguing foreign land.

"When it started, China was coming out of a cultural revolution and just opening itself up to the West," explains the garden's executive director Kathy Scanlan. "And now, some 20 years later, it is a burgeoning world power. It's very significant."

But the age-old Asian mystery remains. Just step onto the raked gravel path, and you'll step into a beautifully intriguing foreign land.

"Entering the garden creates an emotional feeling," says Mark Grant, garden manager of the Seattle Chinese Garden Society. "The ever-green bamboos form a natural covered walkway, creating a feeling of security, like being wrapped up in a blanket."

Following the Sichuan style—lush, green, broad-leaved, and ever-green—the Seattle Chinese Garden features a pond, a rushing gorge, and a lake. Look closely and you'll notice that the water is not clear. Not a sign of neglect, but rather a purpose-built characteristic.

"The Chinese choose opaque water [preferably containing algae and silt], because if the water is clear it won't reflect the plants and trees surrounding it," explains Grant.

Around the pond you'll find reeds, lily pads, cattails, and duckweed. And in the pond, you may find a fish or two, if you're lucky. You may also discover living, breathing creatures in the tree trunks!

"In the winter, look for trunk shapes," says Grant. "The Chinese often chose trees that resemble an old man or woman to create a human form within the garden."

Another Chinese element you will find here is the art of integrating rocks into the garden.

"When stones are integrated into the pathways, a visitor walking through is more connected to nature," explains Grant. "You are walking amongst the garden instead of keeping the garden a separate experience."

And each stone's shape is chosen for a reason.

"The flat stones tend to give people a feeling of relaxation whereas the more prominent or pointed stones send messages of energy or power."

What:
Seattle Chinese Garden

Where:
South Seattle Community College (North Campus behind Garden Center)
6000 16th Ave SW
www.seattle-chinese-garden.org
206.282.8040

When:
Daylight hours year-round (please be aware that the garden will be under construction, changing and growing in the coming years)

Price:
Free; the college also offers free, guided tours

Tiptoe past the flowering purple plumbago. Witness the golden yellow leaves of the Gingko biloba (which they say can make you smarter). Or take in the vanilla scent of the Sarcococca roscifolium. You just might forget you're in West Seattle altogether.

"Visiting the Seattle Chinese Garden is a good way for people to immerse themselves in Chinese culture," says Scanlan. "We tell visitors to come and 'take the West Seattle Bridge to China.'"

RECREATION

25 | Trail Run at Lincoln Park

Looking for a jogging route off the beaten path? Lace up your running shoes and head to Lincoln Park for trail running that rivals some of the area's best venues.

When treadmills make you feel cooped up or you need a break from the pavement, getting into the trees and onto the trail can make for a more inspired workout. Trail running is a growing sport that combines the natural environment of hiking with the daily routine of running. Mix in some scampering squirrels and the shelter of 100-year-old cedar trees, and the endorphins seem even better.

Some compare the transition from road or gym running to trail running as going from automatic to manual. If you like to drive, you'll really love the difference. Your mind and body are more interactive with your surroundings, providing a challenge and an inspiration. But you do need to watch your footing as well as look out for other people and animals you approach on the trail.

At Lincoln Park, take trail #4 down the switchbacks to the beach, or stay on top of it all and weave multiple figure-eight patterns through the trees on level ground. With over 5 miles of trails and many combinations of trails a mile long or less, runners can create numerous routes and easily cover a lot of ground.

Serious trail runners can even train to compete in the grueling 50-mile ultra runs, making marathoners look lax. Thankfully, pounding the trail is gentler on your body than pounding the pavement.

When trail running, the mind and body interact more with the surroundings, providing challenge and inspiration.

How do you get going? Many sports require tons of gear and big investments, but trail running is low maintenance. Whether this is your first shot at running or you're an experienced runner looking for new terrain, all you need are three essentials: energy, good shoes, and water. The last two items are both available Nortwest-style. Local footwear manufacturer Montrail (www.montrail.com) was one of the first to create trail running shoes and local hydration expert Playtpus (www.platypushydration.com) designs bottles and packs made for the trail.

Lighting your path is also recommended on early morning and evening jaunts—wouldn't want roots or rocks to pop out of the dark and ruin your run. With a shady tree canopy and short days during our long winters, many trail runners opt to don a lightweight headlamp to il-luminate the path.

And for the ladies (or those carrying large wads of cash), you may also want a whistle or hand-held mace. It's always best to run with a partner or a four-legged friend, but when the option simply isn't there, you can still be prepared.

For everything you need to know about the sport, visit the website for the All American Trail Running Association (AATRA) at www.trailrunner.com.

Then get outside and try trail running for yourself at Lincoln Park. Douglas firs, furry fauna, and plenty of trails await.

What:
Trail Run

Where:
Lincoln Park
8011 Fauntleroy Way SW
www.cityofseattle.net/parks/
Environment/Trails/lincoln-map.htm
206.684.4122

When:
Year-round

Price:
Free; BYOS (bring your
own shoes)

26 | Skate at Southgate

When outdoor skating or roller-blading the beach is out of the question due to rain and windy weather, you might want to wait before hanging up those skates.

Skating's always in season at Southgate Roller Rink. And there's more now on offer than what you've seen there before.

A local fixture for almost 80 years, the rink still rents standard quad skates and does the Hokey Pokey, but it has also evolved with the times by reviving roller derby and introducing an inline skate racing team.

The Rat City Rollergirls, who call Southgate home, include four roller derby teams—the Derby Liberation Front, the Sockit Wenches, Grave Danger, and the Throttle Rockets—all made up of local women with wit, guts, and insurance.

"Roller derby is a competitive contact sport, so our girls have to be insured," says roller girl Darth Skater, captain of the Throttle Rockets. "But it's so much fun, there's really a buzz about it. Our tryouts are packed and we even have a waiting list."

According to Darth, the roller derby bouts (or competitions) are the hottest ticket in town. "Our bouts sell out in three hours!" she exclaims.

But if you're not about to bout roller derby-style and are ready for something more refined, Southgate also offers an inline skate team. With upwards of 50 members, the Southgate Speed Team features racers of all abilities ranging from age 4 to 55—a good percentage of whom are invited to compete in meets nationally and worldwide.

"Our kids race at meets all over the U.S.," says owner, manager, and coach Francine Tamaccio. "And if they are really good, high-caliber skaters, they are invited to international competitions."

Tamaccio has kept the tradition of working for her family's business, which is also the oldest roller rink in Washington, since age 16.

"We have a class to introduce the basics of how we work as team," encourages Tamaccio. "You don't have to be good to start with. The object is to teach you."

And not only does the sport teach participants how to be better, faster skaters—it also teaches some lessons for life.

"Kids learn to be part of team, to compete, and to practice sportsmanship," she says. "They can go as far as they want to go—from beginner skater all the way through to international competition."

Because the team is open to all ages, the speed-skating team is also a great option for active families who want the convenience and pleasure of being and exercising together.

So whether you're a gal who wants to get down and dirty with roller derby or you have a family of four looking for fun, friendly competition, stop by Southgate next time you roll through the neighborhood.

What:
Roller Derby & Speed Skating

Where:
Southgate Roller Rink
9646 17th Avenue SW
www.southgaterollerrink.com
206.762.4030

Roller Derby League
www.ratcityrollergirls.com

When:
Call or visit the respective sites for session times and try-outs

Prices:
See the websites

27 | *Go Four Wheelin'*

Ever been four-wheelin'? Now's your chance to double the fun of bike riding (or quadruple the fun of unicycling) and get into a four-wheeled, pedal-powered go-kart.

Located on Harbor Avenue just north of the West Seattle Bridge, Pedal Pedal Go Kart rents several four-wheeled vehicles by the hour for jaunts to Alki and beyond. The bikes are quiet, affordable, and pretty good exercise, too. No ATVs here—the only motor running this thing is the one revving up inside you.

In fact, owner Danny Atteberry says his customers are surprised at the amount of exercise they get from pedaling his rigs.

"It is exercise, but it's fun exercise," smiles Atteberry. "That's what everybody tells me when they're done—'now that was fun.'"

An old English sheep dog named Fizzy supervises while Atteberry gets you geared up on your own four-wheeler. Helmets are available on request, and Atteberry assures the vehicles are very safe.

"We've never had one tip yet," he nods.

Actually, many parents bring their kids riding with them by hitching one of the rental trailers to the back. Pedal Pedal Go Kart offers two 2-seat trailers. Besides the kids, you'd be surprised at some of the passengers.

> *An old English sheep dog named Fizzy supervises while Atteberry gets you geared up on your own four-wheeler.*

"I've rented them to guys who want to tow their girlfriends around," explains Atteberry. "There was also a woman in here the other day that towed me around to simulate what it would be like towing her 140-pound dog!"

But Pedal Pedal Go Kart isn't just about vehicles. The owner is part of the experience as well.

A colorful character, Atteberry has

many more passions than just four wheelers. He also repairs bicycle gear, sews, and custom-designs leather goods. So you can get your busted chaps stitched up and ready to roll by the time you're back from your ride. If the bikers only knew, they'd be lined up in front of Atteberry's shop on Thursday nights instead of Alki Tavern.

Jokes aside, these four-wheeled bikes are great for the whole family. So make like the Flintstones and head on down. The kids' eyes will widen while the wheels turn and, best of all, this fun is fully human-powered.

What:
Four-Wheel Biking

Where:
Pedal Pedal Go Karts
(look for "Danny's
Leather" sign)
3310 Harbor Ave SW
206.932.5792

When:
Year-round (weather
permitting); call before
you come

Price:
$5/hour

Seattle cityscape through Westside eyes (and a glass of chardonnay) at Salty's On Alki.

DINING

From tasty Thai to Mai Tais with a kick to traditional standbys that are part and parcel of West Seattle, great dining options in the neighborhood have gone from rare to well done in recent years. Discover for yourself these 23 places to nibble, sip, indulge, and enjoy.

Alki Ave SW

Harbor Ave SW

35

29

39

Admi 36 Way SW

43

31

28

63rd

California Ave SW

West Seattle Bridge

46

42

33

49

47

32

Beach Drive SW

30

SW Alaska St

40

45

51

44

41

37

35th Ave SW

Delridge Way

48

SW Morgan St

Fauntleroy Way SW

16th Ave SW

Fauntleroy Ferry
Terminal ■

34

SW Roxbury St

38

28 | Taste History at the Homestead

Stroll along 61st Avenue just a block off of Alki and you can't help but notice the neatly trimmed lawn. Look a little closer, and you'll discover an original log carriage house nestled beneath towering trees older than Seattle itself.

A bit of history in every bite, the Homestead lies just steps away from the birth-place of Seattle at Alki Point.

Step inside as the wooden floor creaks beneath your feet and catch the glimmer of antique chandeliers flickering in the light of a blazing beach rock fireplace. Touch the exposed timber beams, take in the scent of pan-fried chicken from the kitchen, and you may feel right at home—that is if you were around in 1904.

Welcome to the Alki Homestead Restaurant, a century-old West Seattle landmark where white lace tablecloths, pink napkins, and silver creamers beckon you to sit down and make yourself comfortable. The ticking, antique Seattle P.I. clock, originally given to newspaper subscribers in the early 1900s and complete with every-so-often pauses, makes time stand still.

A bit of history in every bite, the Homestead lies just steps away from the birthplace of Seattle at Alki Point—where the Denny party landed a 60-ton schooner called the *Exact* and rowed ashore on Nov. 13, 1851.

Due to transportation difficulties (something we can still identify with today), Alki Point did not grow like other areas of Seattle and sustained only a small "colony" of settlers. Among these first brave West Seattleites were Mr. and Mrs. William J. Bernard, a couple who loved camping in the area. The Bernards decided to pitch their tent for good in 1902 and began building their new home, which is now the Alki Homestead Restaurant.

Mrs. Bernard is rumored to have carried stones from the beach to create the magnificent fireplace—the warm heart and soul of the home.

To this day, yesteryear is ever present at the Homestead—and even the clientele adds to the historic atmosphere.

"I've heard some customers talk about how they used to take the trolley to Colman Pool," says hostess Autumn Nettey.

From the conversation to the cuisine, many compare the Homestead experience to "going to dinner at Grandma's house."

The Homestead offers a variety of entrées, but regulars seem to enjoy a piece (or five) of the famous pan-fried chicken along with their slice of Seattle history. The all-you-can-eat chicken is served family style with mashed potatoes, vegetables, and a boat of giblet gravy. The meal also includes a hearty cup of soup, a salad, a warm basket of fresh-baked biscuits, and berry jelly. The homestead also offers wine, beer, and a full bar.

For serious comfort food, there's no better fit than a feast inside this toasty, century-old log home. You might even want to stake a claim there.

What:
Alki Homestead

Where:
2717 61st Ave SW
206.935.5678

When:
Wed–Sat 5–10 pm
Sunday 3–8:30 pm

Price:
Entrées run $9.25–$15

29 | Salty's Weekend Brunch

What do you do with 300 pounds of Dungeness crab, 200 dozen oysters, 15 cases of fruit, and 30 pounds of chocolate? Maybe feed a few pro linebackers? Nah, West Seattleites would rather keep it in the neighborhood and call it their own.

Welcome to Salty's weekend brunch—a festival of food with a view.

Each Saturday and Sunday morning, the Salty's crew comes early to assemble the biggest, and arguably the best, brunch in town. The impressive selection features a carving station, a succulent seafood spread, made-to-order crepes, omelets, pasta, an array of salads, breakfast entrées, and desserts. Just sampling a bite of everything offered is nearly impossible in one sitting.

While crab legs, oysters, and eggs benedict top the most popular list, the swirling three-tier chocolate fountain is the crowd favorite (for entertainment value).

"We're the only ones who have a chocolate fountain for brunch, and I like it so much I chose to have one at my own wedding reception," beams Executive Chef Dan Thiessen.

> **"When it comes to traditional weekend brunches, there's nothing like it in Puget Sound."**
>
> Dan Thiessen
> Executive Chef

The fountain of streaming chocolate resembles a cake but rotates in a mesmerizing, mouth-watering fashion. Skewers are available with a medley of fruit, macaroons, and rice crispy treats for dipping. Kids get a kick out of the Willy Wonka factor and adults turn into kids at the sight of it. One woman is even rumored to have dipped and filled her coffee mug in the chocolaty cataract.

Salty's is renowned for its big Sunday spread, but it's also known for continuing (and building) a weekend morning tradition that others have left behind.

"When it comes to traditional weekend brunches, there's nothing like it in Puget Sound," says Thiessen. "In the past, there were a lot of big city hotel-style brunch affairs, but with the trend of hotels getting out of the restaurant business, these brunches have gone away."

And since true weekend brunches are tough to find in Seattle, West Seattleites are lucky to have this one so close to home. In fact, Chef Thiessen has a hint for locals.

"Everybody knows about Salty's Sunday brunch," explains Thiessen. "But our Saturday brunch is a local secret. When it's impossible to get a reservation for Sunday, say, for example, in the summer, the locals go for Saturday instead."

According to Thiessen, the Saturday brunch has a special local feel, where people are more relaxed and less formal, coming more on the spur of the moment.

"We see a lot of familiar faces on Saturday," he smiles. "It's something that our employees talk about with their friends, and clients mention to their hairdressers. Very word of mouth."

So impress your out-of-towners with the virtually endless options or take a good friend for a special treat. Whatever your occasion, this bountiful brunch is the place to be.

What:
Salty's Weekend Brunch

Where:
Salty's on Alki
1936 Harbor Ave SW
www.saltys.com
206.937.1600

When:
Saturday 9:30 am–1 pm
Sunday 9 am–2 pm

Price:
Adults $28.95
Seniors $20.95
Children 5–9 $11.95
4 & under free

30 | *Dial into West 5 Lounge*

Take a stroll through the Alaska Junction and you'll notice an intriguing sign. Strapping red bulbs contrast with the black backdrop of the new West 5 Lounge, harkening back to a quality and comfort found on storefronts and in restaurants decades ago.

A proverbial sign of the times, West 5 is a space where a new generation of West Seattleites meet for old-fashioned fun. A gathering place unlike many that have given way to neon signs and a sort of sameness.

> *West 5 is a space where a new generation of West Seattleites meet for old-fashioned fun.*

"We were looking to do something different without being a theme bar," says co-founder Dave Montoure.

Montoure and business partner Dean Overton, both born and raised in West Seattle, recently gave up their corporate lifestyles to open West 5 Lounge. In his other life, Overton worked as a veteran marketing executive for a leading record label, while Montoure traveled the globe as an Internet tech for a major shipping company.

And this new breed of West Seattle proprietor finds value in the neighborhood's past.

A "Certified Original West Seattle Establishment," the West 5 takes its name from the old "935" West Seattle telephone prefix. If you lived here, you were a "WE5." If you lived in Ballard, your prefix started with an "SU" for Sunset Ave. Queen Anne was "AT" for Atwater. You get the picture—these guys are hip to Seattle history.

"There's a lot of West Seattle memorabilia," says Overton. "It has an early '60s feel from the era of the Seattle World's Fair."

The owners drew on local resources from tabletops to personnel to outfit the place with the proper look and feel. They obtained the pink, neon cocktail sign from the old Admiral Benbow Inn, where they also found their favorite bartender Joann. They also purchased an old oil painting from the former Vann's restaurant.

And the signature signage? The owners took a liking to a sign in an old Bette Davis movie, similar to the Merchant's Café sign in Pioneer Square, and they had to have it. A custom sign maker produced the red-bulbed beauty.

West 5 is a non-smoking establishment that Overton characterizes as a "good, clean cocktail lounge." And as the website states, it's a place for "those merry souls who make drinking a pleasure; who achieve contentedness long before capacity; and who, whenever they drink, prove able to carry it, enjoy it, and remain gentlemen." And gentlewomen, of course.

The bar features a notable wine list and signature drinks such as the West 5 mai tai, the citrus currant drop, and the Chartreuse martini. And the kitchen offers up American bistro-style cuisine and creative comfort food (try the crowd favorite: mac n' cheese).

Step into the new generation of West Seattle class while tasting a bit of the neighborhood's past at West 5 Lounge.

What:
West 5 Lounge

Where:
4539 California Ave SW
www.westfive.com
WE5-1966 (206.935.1966)

When:
Monday–Friday 4 pm–midnight
Saturday Noon–1 pm
Sunday Noon–11 pm

Price:
Drinks run $2.50–$9.00
Entrées run $5–$12.00

Check the website for happy hour specials

31 | Hit the Beach at the Bamboo Bar

When soggy winter weather's got you down or you're ready to celebrate the summertime sunshine, step into West Seattle's tribute to all things tropical: the Bamboo Bar & Grill.

This beachy café on Alki serves up everything you can imagine—and does it island-style. From the signature Bamboo mai tais to tasty pupus (meaning appetizers in Hawaiian), there's enough island hospitality to make anyone a Westside castaway for good.

It's only fitting that Seattle's one true beach boardwalk community also has a beach bungalow-type bar and grill. And whether you sit outside on the surfside patio in summer months or you need somewhere to warm up on a rainy winter day, the Bamboo instills a real beach feel.

You can't help but do a little hula when you see the tiki torches and the airbrushed conch and surf mural by local artist Richard Garcia. And bar manager Zac Russell will make you feel like you stepped straight into the movie *Cocktail* with his shakin', stirrin', and generally entertaining back bar antics. In fact, Russell was recently awarded "Master Mixologist" by Seattle's *Evening Magazine*.

The exotic fare only furthers the experience. The Bamboo Bar & Grill offers specialty drinks such as the Hurricane Alki and the Jamaica Me Crazy as well as tasty dishes like salmon vin blanc and the chef's favorite barbecue ribs.

> *It's only fitting that Seattle's one true beach boardwalk community also has a beach bungalow-type bar and grill.*

Lighter appetites, can't go wrong with an order of the spicy but sweet coconut shrimp paired with a tall, frosty foo-foo drink, umbrella and all. But not everything on the menu is equatorial however. They also serve burgers, pasta, hot sandwiches, and steaks.

While you're drinking and dining, keep your ears open for island sounds, as the Bamboo Bar also offers live Hawaiian-style tunes and Polynesian musical acts from around town. The bar and grill also offers breakfast on the weekend and features 14 TVs mounted throughout for sports fans. So come rain or shine, stop by the Bamboo Bar. It's a little bit of Alki aloha, served up West Seattle-style.

What:
Bamboo Bar & Grill

Where:
2806 Alki Ave SW
Seattle, WA 98116
206.937.3023

When:
Summer hours are
Monday–Friday 11 am–2 am
Saturday & Sunday 9 am–2 am

The rest of the year, the bar
closes at 1 am daily

Price:
Drinks run from $3–$6.75
Entrées run from $7.25–$19.95

32 | Thai's In Bloom at Buddha Ruksa

At the end of the West Seattle Bridge, on the corner of 36th and Genesee, a beautiful, little red restaurant is in bloom.

Welcome to Buddha Ruksa Thai Cuisine.

Pronounced "poot-ta ruck-suw," the name signifies a Thai flower similar to the gladiola. It translates literally to "safe and well under the protection of Buddha." The elegant

> *The name signifies a Thai flower similar to the gladiola and translates literally to "safe and well under the protection of Buddha."*

red blossom is also the favorite flower of His Majesty King Bhumipol Adulyadej of Thailand, whom the restaurant honors by choosing this name.

Along with the flower come royalty, simplicity, and some of the most uniquely prepared Thai food in the neighborhood.

Buddha Ruksa, founded by Anucha "Nui" Onongard and Michael Hootman, opened in January of 2003. Hootman is a Boeing employee with a love for food and a knack for the business side of the venture. Onongard hails from Lopburi, Thailand, just north of Bangkok. He provides years of experience in Thai restaurants as well as a handful of family recipes.

Onongard moved to Seattle in 1993. He first worked for a Thai restaurant in West Seattle and then served and managed for nearly eight years at the Noodle Studio on Broadway. A resident of West Seattle's Pigeon Hill neighborhood, Onongard purposely built his restaurant just minutes away from his home.

The restaurateur chose West Seattle for two reasons. "Restaurant work requires many hours, and I wanted work to be close to home," he says. "Also, West Seattle is a very good neighborhood with sweet people and a real community feel."

The menu is inspired largely by Onongard's mother, who still resides in Thailand. "My mom is a very good cook," grins the proud son. "My sister Anita moved over here to be my cook and uses those same recipes."

Sure, Buddha Ruksa serves your typical swimming rama and multi-colored curries, but the presentation is impeccable (check out the gorgeous garnishes) and there are also a few of "mom's" items here you won't find on other Thai menus. For example, two appetizers straight from the Onongard home. Prawns in a Blanket are garlic-and-pepper-marinated prawns wrapped in a spring roll, deep- fried golden brown, and served with a sweet garlic-chili sauce. Kra-Thong-Tong features golden pastry cups filled with curried ground chicken, shrimp, and vegetables, and is served with a cucumber salad.

Besides everyone's favorite pad thai, Onongard says the crispy garlic chicken sautéed with basil is a real hit. With a new special every week, Onongard aims to keep things fresh and interesting while experimenting with new flavors and styles one week at a time.

The diverse flavors of salty, spicy, sweet, and sour only complement the Zen simplicity of Buddha Ruksa's traditional Thai decor. So check out the little restaurant named after the beautiful flower. Chances are you'll leave your meal also feeling "safe and well."

What:
Buddha Ruksa Thai Cuisine

Where:
3520 SW Genesee St
www.buddharuksa.com
206.937.7676

When:
Tuesday–Friday 11 am–10 pm
Saturday & Sunday 4–10 pm

Price:
Entrées from $5.95–$9.50

33 | Get Connected at Hotwire

DINING

Turn-of-the-century brick walls. Age-old (and always enticing) aromas of grinding coffee. Classically delicious cinnamon rolls. And cutting-edge computer technology?

Discover Hotwire Online Coffeehouse—a coffeehouse that connects the rich flavor of West Seattle history with modern-day convenience.

Sip your steaming beverage in the intimate European-style café while reading your favorite online morning paper. Venture outside to people-watch post office-goers in the mini courtyard. Or familiarize yourself with local painters and photographers in this budding neighborhood art scene.

"It's just a great place to relax and take a break," says founder Lora Vickrey. "A customer once told me that coming to Hotwire is like 'taking a deep breath and being able to let it out here.'"

Maybe it's that much needed "time out" that stopping here for coffee seems to satisfy—but taking a moment to soak up the cozy ambience of days past is also key.

Built in 1910, Hotwire's home has been a part of West Seattle history for close to a century. The friendly little brick building is located on the same site as the original Seattle Lighting Company, and the coffeehouse itself used to be the company's carriage house. Humans have replaced horses and computers have replaced carriages, but history, scented by hazelnut lattes, is still in the air.

> *A coffeehouse that connects the rich flavor of West Seattle history with modern-day convenience.*

Hotwire roasts its own coffee, offering eleven single-origin varieties and a custom-roasted espresso blend. Loose-leaf teas are also available. For a nibble, try the fresh Alki Bakery cookies or indulge in a heated, butter-iced cinnamon roll.

Computer offerings include four machines with DSL, a network plug-in for laptops, a variety of Microsoft office products, a laser printer, and a fax machine. Classes and "study sessions" are free of charge and include a college student study from 2-8 pm on Sundays. Free Internet classes take place every Wednesday from 1 to 2 p.m. followed by kids' night from 6 to 9 p.m.

In addition to coffee and computers, the café also offers an ongoing art show. A rotating exhibit of local artwork, featuring a new artist each month, graces the exposed brick walls and is usually kicked off with a reception.

So if you have out-of-town visitors dying to check their email on a fast machine or if you simply need a spot to hang out and unwind, hit Hotwire for culture, caffeine, and a connection, to the present and past.

What:
Get Connected at Hotwire

Where:
Hotwire Online Coffeehouse
4410 California Ave SW
www.hotwirecoffee.com
206.935.1510

When:
Monday–Friday 7am–9pm
Saturday 8am–8pm
Sunday 8am–6pm

Call ahead for seasonal
hour changes.

Price:
The first 15 minutes of
Internet access are free with
purchase; after that it's 10
cents/minute.

34 | Hop Off at Endolyne Joe's

DINING

Have a hankering for breakfast at the end of the day? Or a continually curious palate you can't keep at bay? Hop off for a bite at Endolyne Joe's—an eclectic neighborhood café named for the last stop (or "end o' the line) on the historic Fauntleroy Trolley No. 2 and its infamous conductor Joe.

Joe himself was said to be quite the ladies' man, with an "insatiable thirst for a good time." Hang around the restaurant's antique

> Joe's, as the locals call it, features a new theme every few months, so the chefs are always whipping up something fresh and unique.

"Last Stop Lounge" long enough, and you may catch a hint of his spirit. The bar itself hails from Wallace, Idaho—a place with a spicy reputation for operating brothels in old frontier hotels all the way up until 1989.

But despite its colorful history, Joe's is a place for good, clean family fun—an atmosphere the owners have instilled in each of their popular eateries.

Started by Chow Foods restaurateurs Peter Levy and Jeremy Hardy, Endolyne Joe's offers a rotating "festival" of food. This successful culinary tradition is also in full swing at the pair's other restaurants, which include the 5 Spot on Queen Anne, Atlas Foods in University Village, Coastal Kitchen on Capitol Hill, the Jitterbug in Wallingford, and the Hi-Life in Ballard.

West Seattle was on Levy and Hardy's radar for quite some time. After seven years of searching, they found a location that "sang a sweet song," and they knew it was the place to call their latest creation home.

Joe's, as the locals call it, features a new theme every few months, so the chefs are always whipping up something fresh and unique. You'll get a taste of everything from the regional American cuisine of the Route 66 theme to the tropical tastes of Key Largo. And the fun doesn't stop with the food. The restaurant also creates the respective festival's atmosphere with music, memorabilia, and décor. Rumor has it one customer even saw a Jackalope there once.

But don't fret over the revolving selection. For creatures of habit who like to find a few good items and stick to 'em, Endolyne Joe's also offers a base menu built for staying power. The left side of the menu features these "always available" choices, while the right side rotates.

Some popular dinner choices are the simply grilled fish of the day, the pork chop supper, and the pan-fried chicken. For lunch, manager Alex Coydan recommends the Rueben on griddled marble rye or the pan-seared mushroom sandwich. And don't forget dessert. Indulge in a classic hot fudge sundae or the fresh fruit crisp.

Endolyne Joe's is jumpin'— open for breakfast, lunch, and dinner seven days a week and also offering what they call "blunch" on the weekends. Next time you're rambling through Fauntleroy, consider hopping off to make a meal at Joe's the last stop of your day, or at least a welcome break along your journey.

What:
Endolyne Joe's

Where:
9261 45th Ave SW
(up the hill from the Fauntleroy Ferry Dock)
www.chowfoods.com
206.937.JOES

When:
Breakfast 8:30 am–3 pm daily
Lunch 11 am–4 pm daily
Dinner 4–10 pm (bar is open 'til midnight)

Note: The restaurant is closed from 3–5 pm on Saturday & Sunday for re-setting

Prices:
Breakfast is $4.75–$8.75
Lunch is $4.50–$10.50
Dinner entrées are $8.50–$20.75

Note: Prices vary with rotating menu "festivals" and daily specials

35 | Dining Out for Life

How often do you go out for dinner? Once a month? Once a week? Once a night? Whatever your restaurant habits may be, one of the best annual excuses to dine out in West Seattle is "Dining Out for Life."

Held every April from Dallas to Philly, Chicago to St. Louis, and right here in West Seattle, Dining Out for Life offers an annual night in good taste where restaurants donate a portion of one night's profits to local AIDS programs. In Seattle's case, proceeds go to the Lifelong AIDS Alliance.

It's a chance to give effortlessly, without going above and beyond your routine, monetarily or time-wise. The only cost to you is your average meal ticket at your favorite area eateries (check the website yearly to see West Seattle's "participating restaurants").

"It's an opportunity to bring our community together, eat good food, and support the fight against AIDS," says events coordinator Jason Johnson.

> **"It's like a big family party. Customers move over at their tables to allow more room for people to sit down and spend money for a successful night."**
>
> Danny Mitchell
> owner of Angelina's

It's also nothing new to active industry leaders in West Seattle. Many of the neighborhood establishments have been doing it for years.

"Angelina's has participated in the event since it began well over a decade ago," says Johnson.

"We have very loyal clientele that come to this event," says Angelina's owner Danny Mitchell. "It's like a big family party. Customers move over at their tables to allow more room for people to sit down and spend money for a successful night."

Some other area restaurants that

have participated in the past are Abbondonza Pizzeria, Buddha Ruksa, Circa, Endolyne Joe's, and Ovio Bistro.

Dining Out for Life has become one of the best loved and well attended fundraisers in the city, supporting the largest AIDS service agency in the Pacific Northwest. Funds raised not only go for prevention education, but also provide direct assistance in the form of housing, food and nutrition services, insurance continuation, transportation, case management, and emergency funding to people living with HIV and AIDS.

As carbon-based life forms dependent on food for survival, we all have to eat anyway. So it doesn't hurt to pick a place that's consciously making an effort to help those in need. And at the same time, by "dining out for life," you're showing support for those restaurants that have sacrificed profits for the priceless gift of giving.

What:
Dining Out for Life

Where:
West Seattle (see website
for participating restaurants)
www.dineoutforlife.org
206.323.DINE

When:
Every year in April
(check site for specific date)

Price:
The normal meal ticket

36 | Ole for the Matador

Ole! Hot happy hour specials and spicy Tex-Mex cuisine have roared like a mad bull onto the Westside scene.

So when you're craving some spice and Tamarindo on ice, throw on your teleguillas (bull-fighting pants), and visit the Matador in its brand new arena.

The West Seattle Junction restaurant and tequila bar is adorned with bull heads, wooden crosses, vibrant "flaming" stained glass, and intricate wrought iron sculpture inside and out.

> *Hot happy hour specials and spicy Tex-Mex cuisine have roared like a mad bull onto the Westside scene.*

With beginnings in Ballard, the Matador was founded by owners Zak Melang and Nate Opper in 2004. After much success, the two set their sites on opening a second location and picked the heart of West Seattle for restaurant numero dos—Matador West.

"I've lived in West Seattle for six years and always wanted to open a place here," explains Opper. "And a lot of people from West Seattle were coming to our Ballard location encouraging us to do the same."

The partners felt the area needed more options to choose from for late night food and drink. They looked at the demographics and determined that, "West Seattle was just screaming for us!"

With two happy hour times—from 4 to 6 p.m. and 10 p.m. to 1 a.m.—patrons can take advantage of tasty nibbles and drinks for not mucho dinero. Two people can sip a margarita each, try tacos and nachos, and walk away full for under $20.

But there's more. The Matador has an entire arena of Tex-Mex apps and entrées, not to mention 50-plus types of tequila—from the $5 shot of Sauza Gold to the $80 Don Julio Reál. In fact, rumor has it that the owners conducted special, in-depth research with visits to the tiny

Mexican town of Tequila where they toured (and sampled) tequila at the Cuervo plant and also the Sauza factory.

Other buenos beverages to sample are the house-made mojito, Sangria, and Tamarindo, which is a fresh tamarind juice margarita with a cinnamon sugar rim and an orange wedge garnish.

Crowd favorites on the food front include the barbecued pulled pork sandwich, carne asada, roasted tomatillo enchiladas, and skillet-seared steak fajitas.

And for dessert? Matador presents the traditional Mexican flan, chocolate soufflé, and the Banana Crown, a delicious mix of bananas and brown sugar rolled up spring-roll style, deep fried, and served with coconut ice cream.

So, if you're hankering for Tex-Mex and tequila, or just hungry for a happenin' happy hour, enter the ring at Matador.

What:
Matador West Restaurant & Tequila Bar

Where:
4546 California Ave. SW
www.matadorseattle.com
206.932.9988

When:
Monday–Friday 4 pm–2 am
Saturday & Sunday 11 am–2 am

Price:
Entrees range from $8.95–$19.95

37 | Eclectic Flavors at Ovio Bistro

DINING

Up for an evening of eclectic entrées, unique drinks, and decadent desserts? Try West Seattle's Ovio Bistro. Pronounced OH-vee-OH, the name stems from the Latin root 'ovum' meaning egg. For owners Ellie and Shing Chin this name symbolized new beginnings in West Seattle and at home as Ellie was expecting a child when the restaurant opened.

Look closely at the restaurant's logo and you'll see that the letters O-V-I-O form a vertical martini glass. Inside, Shing will gladly fill such a glass for you while you take in the water view from the upscale cocktail area. Ballard residents, the couple formerly co-owned the popular Market Street Grill and has since sold their interest to start anew on the Westside, bringing their great chef, Eddie Montoya, along with them.

"We live in Ballard but have always loved West Seattle," explains owner Ellie Chin. "We love the feeling of neighborhood. That's why we didn't choose Belltown or another city location." The bistro was chosen as the "Best New Restaurant 2003" by Seattle Magazine and offers good healthy servings of fine fare.

"It's Belltown quality at a neighborhood price," remarks Shing Chin.

With seating for over 100, a bar and cocktail lounge, and a separate room to host private parties, Ovio offers a haven for large groups as well as intriguing cuisine for large appetites.

A favorite seafood starter is the crisp-fried blue corn calamari with lemon habanero tartar and green chili vinaigrette. Some of Ovio's most popular entrées are the crispy fried chicken with bacon cheddar mashed potatoes, and the seared rare ahi tuna served over sticky rice and bok choy with lemongrass beurre blanc and soy mustard glaze for dipping. Perfect for meat lovers, the grilled dry-aged rack of lamb features tomato-feta gratin, lamb sausage, and kumquat preserves.

> **"It's Belltown quality at a neighborhood price."**
>
> Shing Chin
> co-owner

Ovio's classy bar and cocktail lounge is the perfect concoction to pair with a dinner entrée or just a good excuse to meet for drinks.

"West Seattle is really discovering the bar," says Ellie Chin. "It's a great meet-and-greet place for friends or business colleagues while watching the ferries go by below."

The full bar offers everything from aged 12-year-old green Chartreuse to a wide selection of ports. The homemade hot buttered rum is a treat come winter, and summer is the prime time to try the passion fruit punch or an Ovio mojito complete with fresh mint syrup made from scratch.

Top your meal off with the warm chocolate and dulce de leche cake or huckleberry cobbler, and your evening will be complete.

But keep your eyes out for new and novel delights as the Ovio menu continually changes—as well it should in a bistro eclectica.

What:
Ovio Bistro Eclectica

Where:
4752 California Ave SW
www.oviobistro.com
206.935.1774

When:
Monday–Thursday 5–10 pm
Friday & Saturday 5–11 pm

Reservations recommended

Price:
Entrées run $14.50–$27.95

38 | Savor the Salvadorian Bakery

Pass this hotspot at night and you may wonder why a bakery draws such a crowd during after-dinner hours. Taste a Salvadorian pupusa—a popular all-day snack—and you'll know why.

Bienvenidos to the Salvadorian Bakery—a Central American place for tasty pastries and more.

"My sister used to own a bakery in El Salvador," explains Ana Castro, who owns the bakery with her sister Aminta Elgin.

But the sisters left the country in the mid '80s due to the war.

"I never thought we'd be doing what we are now. When we came, we didn't know any people or the language," Castro recalls. "But she was eager and kept telling me we should we do what we did in El Salvador."

> "Our store has brought together all kinds of ethnic groups—Central American, Mexicans, Americans.
>
> Ana Castro
> co-owner

So the two went to school to learn English while working at the same time.

"We had no money and thought 'how are we going to this?'" reflects Castro. "So we figured out how to mortgage our houses and start the business."

They began with a tiny bakery in 1996 that has since grown and moved and grown some more. And the client-base has also grown to include more than just Salvadorian supporters.

"We are not just a restaurant for Salvadorian people, but for everyone," beams Castro. "Our store has brought together all kinds of ethnic groups—Central American, Mexicans, Americans. People come from all over, from Tacoma to Bellingham."

The pastries, pupusas, and fried plantains speak for themselves. And if you're trying the Salvadorian Bakery for the first time, there are a couple popular specialties to sample. Try the quesadilla for example. This is not your typical tortilla with melted cheese. It's actually a breakfast pastry resembling a large, flat-top muffin.

"In my country, a quesadilla is a sweet pastry made with milk, sour cream, margarine, cheese, rice flower, wheat flower, and sugar, sprinkled with sesame seeds," says Castro, spoken like a true baker. "Many people compare it to corn bread."

Other popular pastries include the empanada de leche, a yummy, doughy pastry prepared with homemade custard, and the semita, a triangular-cut wheat pastry filled with pineapple and molasses.

And if you need a heartier breakfast, chorizo con huevo (chorizo sausage with eggs, beans, tortillas, and cream) will do the trick. The bakery also offers lunch and dinner—try the guisadas, a Salvadorian stew. The snacks, however, are what keep many coming back.

Crowd favorites include the chicharron pupusa (a handmade tortilla filled with seasoned pork), the tamale de elote (a sweet corn tamale topped with sour cream), and platano frito con frijoles y crema (fried plantain with beans and cream).

And don't forget dessert. The tres leches cake is such a special treat, many customers special order it for weddings and birthdays.

What:
Salvadorian Bakery

Where:
1719 SW Roxbury
206.762.4064

When:
Monday–Friday 6 am–9 pm
Saturday & Sunday 7 am–9 pm

Price:
Meals run $1.95–$12.95

And the best part is that almost every meal on the menu is available all day long. So swing on by Roxbury morning, noon, and night for the unique taste of El Salvador, and more.

39 | Celtic Swell: Irish Pub with Westside Twist

DINING

Walk by and catch the scent of steaming shepherd's pie. Witness a pair of brothers toasting two perfectly poured pints of Guinness. Hear familiar folksongs sung in strong, smiling accents, and watch West Seattleites do a little jig in celebration of the neighborhood's first (and long-awaited) authentic Irish pub—the Celtic Swell on Alki.

Featuring live Irish music, weekend brunch, lunch, dinner, and some serious pub grub, the Celtic Swell offers traditional Irish hospitality and a range of classic dishes, such as Irish stew, sausage rolls, and potato leek soup. The menu also features typical Irish foods with a twist like the Harp tempura fish and chips and the Guinness ice cream developed for Celtic Swell by Snoqualmie Gourmet.

And though it's a pub, because it's Irish style, the Swell caters to families, as well as friends and late-night loungers.

"The pub scene in Ireland is very social for all ages. It's a tradition—a place to hang out and have a chat," says owner Gareth Hughes.

How did Celtic Swell emerge on the shores of Alki? 'Twas a tale of true love for owners Gareth and Joleen Hughes.

> "The pub scene in Ireland is very social for all ages. It's a tradition—a place to hang out and have a chat."
>
> Gareth Hughes
> co-owner

The two met at an Irish bar (seriously) on St. Patrick's (of all days). Joleen was wearing the Irish national rugby team jersey and Gareth simply had to talk to her. The couple's been inseparable since.

As the relationship progressed, Joleen convinced Gareth to take his first vacation ever, destination Maui. Whiling away the hours at this island paradise, the couple hooked up with an Irish friend who ran a successful pub in Wailea, and they were inspired to create their own Irish oasis on the beach back home. What could be better than sipping a pint while watching the waves in West Seattle?

"We were married in Maui a year later and solidified our plans to open our own Irish bar on the beach at Alki," smiles Joleen. "We wanted to work together and make our own stamp on life and at the same time create a place that was somewhere people could congregate until late into the night."

And the couple made it so.

But for the Hughes', who are also Alki residents, the Celtic Swell is more than a pub with a view. It's a way of life. An excuse to get together with family and friends. A place to have fun or "craic" (as fun is called in Gaelic). A tribute to the joy of living— beach-style.

"We felt it was necessary to have a place in West Seattle that people could go to after a movie to grab a beer without going downtown," says Joleen. "It's a place where you don't always know who exactly will be there, but you'll always run into someone you know."

What:
Celtic Swell Irish Pub

Where:
2722 Alki Avenue SW
www.CelticSwell.com
206.932.7935

When:
Monday 4 pm–2 am
Tuesday–Friday 11am–2 am
Saturday & Sunday 9 am–2 am

Price:
Entrées run from $8–$18 with nightly specials at market price

Drinks run from $3–$20 (for a shot of high-end Irish whisky)

40 | Indian Magic at the Maharaja

You may have walked by it a million times. And if you were lucky, maybe the door opened at just the right moment to let the distinct aroma of the tandoori clay oven lure you in. But if not, it's time to experience the unexpected magic of the Maharaja.

This "house of exotic Indian food" adds unique spice to the neighborhood in more ways than one.

Curry, naan, vindaloo—yum! This "house of exotic Indian food" brings the taste of Northern India right here to West Seattle. Described on the takeout menu as a "festival of Indian curries," this enticing spot adds unique spice to the neighborhood in more ways than one.

"Everything is homemade and cooked to order," says manager Gary Virk. "It's authentic and healthy with all kinds of different spices."

Just pick the type of meat you prefer and whether you'd like it mild, medium, or spicy, and the wait staff can recommend an appropriate dish. Some crowd favorites include chicken tikka masala and lamb saag.

And if you're a vegetarian or vegan, you will see that the Maharaja is a great place to be. The options are numerous, and the flavors robust. No watered-down boring veg food here. Just try the vegetable korma and see.

A family-run business, the Maharaja Cuisine of India began well over a decade ago. And the cooking is passed down from generation to generation. Owner Sam Virk, with help from his brother Gary, sees that each dish is prepared with traditional Indian techniques.

But the genuine, flavorful food is just one intriguing aspect of this Indian-influenced Junction icon. There is more to be found in the lounge.

Referred to by regulars as "The Maha," the discreet neighborhood watering hole in the back features signature drinks, a charismatic staff, and memorable patrons with whom to make merry. The Maha's jukebox has some of the best selections in town and is sure to entice you out onto the dance floor, unless one of the regulars asks you out there first.

Stop by on a weekend night for bartender Don Bogie's red and delicious "Washington Apple" cocktail or a refreshing mangorita, and you're sure to have a fine time at this special, secret Westside hangout.

So whether you're looking for a spicy new curry or the distinct taste of tandoori, or an interesting way to spice up your nightlife, let the magic of "Maha" lure you in.

What:
Maharaja Cuisine of India

Where:
4542 California Ave SW
206.935.9443

When:
Restaurant hours are
11:30 am–10:30 pm daily

Lounge hours are
11:30 am–close daily

Price:
Entrées run $7.95–$15.95
Drinks run $1.50–$7.50

41 | Elliott Bay Brews Neighborhood Tradition

Pale ale lovers ask for Alembic by name. But you can't go wrong with No Doubt Stout. Grab a Luna for a heck-of-a Hef. And if you're just in the mood for good, hearty pub food, waiter Tim Pew will personally deliver it to your table with his signature three-fingered, centrifugal serving style (while whistling, if you're lucky).

Welcome to Elliott Bay Brewery—West Seattle's one and only neighborhood brew pub.

Filled to the gills for dinner and lunch, Elliott Bay is a favorite meeting place for a tight-knit community of families and friends.

"We felt a brewery was an opportunity waiting to happen," reflects owner Todd Carden. "Everybody who was moving into the neighborhood wanted to raise their kids in a place with a real sense of community. We captured that audience as the community regentrified here."

But the brewery has also formed a community of its own.

> **"Customers love the food and beer, but they also just love being here."**
>
> Liz Knutson
> general manager

"I've watched many friendships form here," smiles general manager Liz Knutson. "One day people will be sitting at the bar not knowing each other, and before long they are helping each other move, or watching each other's pets when they go on vacation."

The brewery opened its doors on July 11, 1997—unwittingly right in the middle of the annual Junction Street Fair. You could almost say they've been slammed ever since. Owners Todd Carden and Brent Norton previously worked at Maritime Pacific Brewing Company, but wanted to brew up their own business on the other side of the bay.

With the help of soon-to-be customers, the two built the oak bar and booths by hand, brewed their first batches, and began hanging local artwork on the exposed brick walls.

Head brewer Doug Hindman helped developed the signature beers, and his work has been recognized in Denver multiple times during the Great American Beer Festival. In 2000 Elliott Bay was awarded a gold medal for the Alembic Pale (named after Norton's sailboat, Jerry Garcia's guitar, and a glass beaker used to distill alcohol). The next year the pub won a gold medal for the Orange Infusion. In 2003, they took home a bronze for the seasonal Demolition Ale (named after the commotion of the Junction sidewalk project at the time of brewing).

Each week Hindman continues to brew small batches of these handcrafted ales in the 7-barrel (200 gallon) brewery.

And though many argue beer is food, Chef Edward "Rocky" Trabue wouldn't want you to miss out on what makes Elliott Bay as good a restaurant as it is a brew pub.

Crowd favorites include the Hoppin Hummus, ahi tacos, and the Brewer's Burger. All burgers are made with Misty Isles Black Angus beef raised on Vashon Island, and the spent grain from the brewing process is used to make the buns.

"Customers love the food and beer, but they also just love being here," nods Knutson.

So whether you come by for a pint, a bite, or both, take the time to relax, unwind, and revel in the tradition-in-the-making brewing up around you.

What:
Elliott Bay Brewery

Where:
4720 California Ave SW
www.elliottbaybrewing.com
206.932.8695

When:
Monday–Saturday 11 am–midnight
Sunday 11 am–11 pm
Happy hour is from 3–6 pm daily

Price:
Signature brews run
$3.75-$4.50 per pint

Entrées run $6.75-$9.95

42 | Luna Park Fun Lives On

On warm summer weekends in West Seattle's early days, Seattleites ferried from downtown in droves to visit Luna Park. "The Coney Island of the West," Luna Park was a fun-filled amusement park built on a pier off Alki, complete with rides, a roller coaster, and calliope music.

> *"Shakes are the big thing here."*
>
> John Bennett
> owner

Closed in 1913, the brightly lit area attraction, which once illuminated Elliott Bay, is just a faint memory. Only the remnants of the pier's original pilings are exposed at low tide. But now, a red neon sign at the end of the West Seattle Bridge leads the way to a 21st-century institution of the same name, attracting a new set of West Seattle fun-seekers.

Welcome to the Luna Park Café—a nostalgic restaurant and living museum that serves up tasty shakes, malt shop-style, and a huge helping of community history.

The walls are adorned with West Seattle artifacts and historic black-and-white photos of the "greatest amusement park in the Northwest."

Built in 1988 by current owner John Bennett, Luna Park Café was made to reflect fun times of the past. "I thought it would be great to open a '50s diner with a jukebox and neighborhood memorabilia," recalls Bennett.

But the décor is just part of the Luna Park draw. All-day breakfast, traditional soda fountain drinks, burgers, and a beer garden keep tummies coming back for good, old-fashioned food.

The egg breakfasts are served three ways—as a "pile," a "hobo," or an omelet. However you take 'em, save room for dessert.

"Shakes are the big thing here," says Bennett. "They're made fresh with Cascade Glacier ice cream and topped with whip and a cherry. We also offer one of the only places in West Seattle to enjoy a beer and a burger in the sunshine outside."

Luna Park's remodeled beer garden, nestled amidst jasmine and clematis, seats 50 diners and offers lots of sunshine when the weather gods wish.

"We've been here for years," reflects Bennett. And people remember Luna Park as a foundation for things like kids' birthdays, meals after soccer games, and great shakes year-round.

"A woman and her 18-year-old son—who was at least 6 feet tall, mind you—came in the other day," smiles Bennett. "The mom pulled out a photo of her tiny son at age two sitting on our kid's coin-operated ride, and the son said to me, 'I'll never forget riding your Bat Mobile.'"

So grab a chocolate shake or ponder the past with relics that line the walls. The same festive atmosphere that once adorned the shores of Alki is on the menu at the Luna Park of today—building new neighborhood memories for kids and grownups alike.

What:
Luna Park Café

Where:
2918 SW Avalon Way
206.935.7250

When:
Sunday–Thursday 7 am–9 pm
Friday & Saturday 7 am–10 pm

Price:
Breakfasts entrées run $4.95–$7.95
Lunch and dinner entrées run
$6.95–$8.50

43 | Pegasus Puts Greek Pizza on a Pedestal

Its name is inspired by a winged horse in Greek mythology. Its specialty is arguably one of the Greeks' best-ever culinary creations. And it's the only place in West Seattle that has been putting pizza on a pedestal for more than 20 years now.

Presenting Pegasus Pizza—a standing tradition on Alki.

"We started the tradition of serving our pizza on pedestals," smiles owner Ted Nicoloudakis. "It keeps the scent of pizza nice and close to the nose, where you can better appreciate it, while leaving plenty of room on the table for wine or beer."

Pegasus opened its doors in 1984 and has been serving up consistently delicious pies ever since. Known for its Greek-style pan-pizza dough, which is made fresh daily, Pegasus pizza is most commonly described as croissant-style—light and flaky. Not too thin. Not too thick.

But rolling out this dough was nothing new even in the early '80s. Rather, it's always run in the family, so to speak.

> "We started the tradition of serving our pizza on pedestals. It keeps the scent of pizza nice and close to the nose."
>
> Ted Nicoloudakis
> owner

According to Nicoloudakis, Greeks invented the pizza. And now in West Seattle, he and his cohorts have spent more than two decades perfecting it.

The crowd favorite is the "Tom's Special," otherwise known as the "House." It's made with feta, mushrooms, green peppers, onions, olives, garlic, tomatoes, spinach, sunflower seeds, and pepperoni. Other popular picks include Greek salad and white spaghetti made with Greek Myzithra cheese.

But pizza is the preference for most

Pegasus-goers, and people come from all over for it.

"We've even had customers from Chicago and New York—famous places for pizza—say it's the best pizza they've ever tried," nods Nicoloudakis. "And here locally, people from islands all over Puget Sound make it a destination. They come to walk the beach, appreciate the view, and enjoy the pizza."

And those who can't stay to savor the flavors in person just pick up a pizza to go—sometimes much farther than home.

"Our customers have said they crave our pizza when they're away on vacation, so we make half-baked pizzas to take on the road," explains manager Clara Doray. "We half-bake the pizza in order to get the dough out of the pan, then the customer finishes baking it wherever they may be."

But nothing matches being there to take in the symphony of activity in the Pegasus kitchen, not to mention the beautiful beach scene.

"Sitting outside for a pizza here in the summer is unbeatable," beams Nicoloudakis. "The food, the view, the people-watching..."

And for some, it's also sentimental.

What:
Pegasus Pizza

Where:
2758 Alki Avenue SW
206.932.4849

When:
Monday–Friday 11:30 am–11 pm
Saturday & Sunday Noon–11 pm

Price:
Pizzas run $9.25–$19.75
depending on size and toppings

"We have a couple who went on their first date here," smiles Doray. "They came to propose here, ate here the night of their wedding, white dress and all, and come back every year for their anniversary."

It's safe to call this couple "regulars." But according to staff, most customers are regulars—putting this unique Greek pizza place on a pedestal of their own.

44 | Real Food, Real Fresh at Mashiko

Enter the door and prepare to explore—a taste of Japan in the heart of West Seattle. From the traditionally trained sushi chef to the fresh albacore, Mashiko is the real deal.

Named after a Japanese town that is known for its ceramics and nearby owner Hajime Sato's home town, Mashiko began to set the local sushi scene while setting the table with the famed pottery.

> *"Some people think you need knowledge to sit at a sushi bar, but it's the opposite. How many restaurants can you consult the chef while he's making your food?"*
>
> Hajime Sato
> owner

But Sato's vision was not to serve sushi on fancy plates. He sought to serve real Japanese cuisine at a really fair price. Sato came to the States as an exchange student, and now he's served the neighborhood sushi for more than a decade. In fact, Mashiko is West Seattle's only Japanese-owned Japanese restaurant.

"Most people just assume I'm not from Japan because I speak good English," smiles Sato.

Sato once served an older Japanese couple a traditional meal and said they were stunned when he not only sat down to speak their language- but also served up time-honored, traditional dishes.

"I was trained as a traditional Japanese chef and will never forget my heritage," reflects Sato. "But I also try new things to continually educate myself."

According to Sato, a sushi chef should prepare food in front of you and accommodate to personal tastes.

"I will make you a very different meal from the person sitting right next to you," says Sato. "It's not a production line."

If it were, the sushi bar would smell fishy. To ensure freshness, the menu continually changes. Sushi connoisseurs opt for the "omakase" (or chef's choice) to sample catch(es) of the day. You wouldn't want to miss out on the fresh eel avo kabocha pumpkin roll when it's available—this way Sato makes sure you won't.

"In Japan, there are no menus or prices. You let the chef decide," he explains.

But if you prefer to order off the menu, crowd favorites include the breaded, flash-fried "Mashiko tuna," the tempura onion and albacore "Temptation Island," and the spicy tuna, cilantro, and avocado "Red Violin."

And if you're a sushi novice, don't fret. Order "Sushi 101" or, better yet, sit at the bar with Sato.

"Some people think you need knowledge to sit at a sushi bar, but it's the opposite," he continues. "How many restaurants can you consult the chef while he's making your food?"

For beginners, manager Chris Collier suggests, "Start with cooked items first. Then when you get comfortable you can move to the ama ebi, raw shrimp with a fried head."

What:
Mashiko Sushi

Where:
4725 California SW
www.sushiwhore.com
206.935.4339

When:
Monday–Thursday 5–9:30 pm
Friday & Saturday 5–11 pm

Price:
Prices vary from one piece of sushi to entire meals; see the website for price listings.

So whether you're a first-timer or a sushi aficionado, come with an open mind and you may be pleasantly surprised. Just follow Sato's rule #10 (found on the menu's front page) that reads: "Don't be afraid to try something new." All guests are also encouraged to check pretentiousness at the door.

"Sure, our presentation is nice, but we're definitely not foo foo," says Sato. "What you'll find here is real food and real people—and of course real fresh fish."

45 | The Scoop on Husky Deli

Anyone who's lived in West Seattle from 1932 until now knows about the dreamy, ice creamy charm of Husky Deli. Whether it's the mountainous scoop of Husky Flake that's part of every local kid's childhood or the Rueben on dark rye that the business crowd craves for lunch, the offerings are as authentic as the smiling proprietor Jack Miller.

But what you might not know about this neighborhood icon is that it helped the community survive tough times while West Seattle's sweet tooth, in turn, kept Husky alive.

According to Miller, the family-run business began when his grandfather Herman Miller, an Indiana cattle breeder, moved from Eastern Washington to Seattle to sell Kelvinator commercial refrigerators in the mid-1920s. Soon after his arrival, the then-named Edgewood Farms Grocery store in West Seattle was up for sale. Miller bought the business in 1932, immediately purchased a Mills ice cream machine, and began making homemade ice cream in the store's front window for all to see.

His store soon became known for a neighborhood treat called the "Husky"—a giant scoop of ice cream dipped in chocolate and rolled in nuts. Miller signed a contract to sell his Huskies to public school lunch programs, which kept his business going through the Depression. In turn, to serve his customers during these hard times, Miller let them run a tab if they could not afford to pay for their groceries. Embraced by the community, this act of kindness earned him loyal customers—while the schoolkids' love for ice cream kept Miller's business churning.

> **"Ice cream still saves the day."**
>
> Jack Miller
> owner

In 1937, Miller changed the name of the store to Husky and trademarked the ice cream. The store became a soda fountain until Miller's sons returned from the WWII, when he converted it to the deli it is today.

"We had a lot of Europeans living in the community," explains Jack.

"As time went on, we became a deli that catered to the customers' requests. We carried things you couldn't find anywhere else."

And Husky, the international deli, was born.

With the world shrinking, many grocery stores now carry these same goods. Still, nothing can replace Husky's commitment to the community. According to Jack, "Ice cream still saves the day."

The place where West Seattleites bought their staples during war times and the Depression continues to build a loyal following.

"It's a treat to have always been here," beams Jack. "When kids we once knew go away and come back years later, they're excited we remember them and know their names. And even though a lot has changed, we're still the same. It's a family-run business and always will be—with 24 grandkids coming up, eight of which already work here."

A life-long gathering place, Husky has a tie to the community that, like their ice cream, is frozen in time.

So if you're looking for a heaping helping of local history and homemade ice cream, stop by Husky Deli for the best scoop in town.

What:
Husky Deli

Where:
4721 California Ave SW
www.huskydeli.com
206.937.2810

When:
Monday–Saturday 9 am–9 pm
Sunday 9 am–7 pm

Price:
A single scoop for $2;
or $3.50 for two

46 | *La Rustica Romantica*

Step into the intimate Italian courtyard. Put your name on the list and wander around back for a glass of Chianti in the cozy, old-country lobby. And get ready for a romantic evening, reminiscent of the Italian Riviera, yet nestled between residences right here on Beach Drive.

> *"La cucina rustica. It's like a rustic kitchen or rustic-style Italian cooking."*
>
> Giulio Pellegrini
> owner

Presenting La Rustica—a "molta romantica" beach bistro.

The name, La Rustica, means "rustic," as the atmosphere suggests, but also refers to the cuisine found within.

"*La cucina rustica,*" passionately explains owner Giulio Pellegrini with gesturing hands. "It's like a rustic kitchen or rustic-style Italian cooking."

Pellegrini opened the bistro's doors in 1996.

"I like the small-town feel of West Seattle," reflects Pellegrini. "That's why we came here."

Pellegrini came from a tiny Italian town called Patrica, south of Rome. At age 19 he crossed the Atlantic to earn a degree in art. He began with painting and sculpture but eventually turned his artistic emphasis from the palette to the palate.

"I taught myself how to cook, and if I didn't understand something, I'd call my mother in Italy to help me," he recalls. "I always wanted to make sure I was keeping it authentic."

Now, as you can see (and certainly taste), Pellegrini's preparations and the environs are exactly that—not to mention artful. His degree came in handy when it was time for décor. Created by Guilio and his children, the restaurant's interior features countless details that resemble his home country: realistic wall cracks, exposed stone masonry, and over-flowing flower vases.

But according to Pellegrini, it's not pretty presentation that packs the house each night. It's hard work each day and engaging the guest each step of the meal.

"Your experience starts the moment you walk in," he describes. "First, you need to find a smile and feel comfortable here. Next, the wait staff should take care of you, and then, finally, comes the food."

But the process begins well before entering the door.

"We are here from nine o'clock in the morning [though they open at 5 pm]," he explains. "My wife Janie is making desserts and tending the flowers. And come June and July, you'll see why—this is one of the best gardens in West Seattle."

He proudly claims Janie's chocolate torte is the best in town. "It just melts in your mouth, literally."

Others say the same about his signature lamb shank.

"Yes, everybody loves the lamb shank," he nods. "I once took it off the menu in summer, as it is not a typical summer dish, but people went crazy. So, it's back."

What:
La Rustica

Where:
4100 Beach Dr SW
206.932.3020

When:
Tuesday–Thursday 5–10 pm
Friday & Saturday 5–10:30 pm
Sunday 5–9:30 pm

Price:
Entrées run $12.95–$29.95

Some of Pellegrini's other people-pleasers include his vitello scampi (veal wrapped in prawns with marsala), filet gorgonzola, and made-to-order cioppino. La Rustica is also known for fresh-baked focaccia and an extensive (all Italian) wine list.

So bring a loved one down to this intimate beach bistro to taste a slice of Italian life, and toast "salute" to West Seattle's own ristorante romantico.

47 | Saunter in for Steak at JaK's Grill

Swagger on in. Your very own mahogany booth awaits you—along with a back bar martini and the finest cut of steak in the neighborhood. Just follow the green neon sign (and your nose) to JaK's Grill.

Named for the first initial of each of the founders' names (Jeff Page and Ken Hughes), JaK's Grill has been a rare find on the Westside since day one.

"We started from humble beginnings," recalls Hughes. "With 10 tables in a small space in Admiral, we were as tiny as you could imagine. But our core philosophy of great steak and great service really helped us grow."

Since the original location in Admiral, JaK's has moved to a spacious spot in the heart of the Junction and opened other locations in Issaquah and Laurelhurst.

"Our vision was to take downtown, white-tablecloth service and the allure of a high-end steakhouse and bring it to the neighborhood at a neighborhood price," says Hughes.

And even with rising meat costs, the value remains. At JaK's, everything's included with your entrée—salad, bread, a side dish, and vegetables, not to mention free parking. Compare it to a similar experience downtown and it's roughly half the price—plus a couple extra ounces a la JaK.

> "You're always going to know somebody here. It feels sort of like a cocktail party."
>
> Ken Hughes
> co-owner

"People come for the steaks," nods Hughes. "We serve 100 percent Nebraska corn-fed beef, aged for 28 days, charbroiled, and finished with our full-flavored steak butter. And the portion sizes are larger than most with a petite weighing in at 10 ounces, and a 'JaK's cut' at 16 ounces—unless you can handle our 21-ounce porterhouse."

The crowd favorite is the filet mignon, followed by the smoked rib eye and the beef skewers specials. But if you have a beef with beef, do not fret. JaK's also serves up wild king salmon, ancho chili grilled prawns with chipotle cream sauce, Caribbean pork medallions, and grilled vegetable specialties. For lighter appetites, burgers and salads are also available.

And the potato portions of a typical meat-and-potatoes meal are a guilty pleasure all their own. In fact, locals ask for the best of both worlds with a garlic mash and potato pancake combo called the "UFO."

Another Westside secret is that, even though JaK's doesn't take reservations, locals can stop by at 5 p.m., put their name on the list with a cell number, and come back later to get right in. And these locals are loyal.

"At least half our guests are regulars, kind of like 'Cheers' in that perspective," smiles Hughes. "You're always going to know somebody here. It feels sort of like a cocktail party."

So whether you're seeking a superior steak dinner, looking to socialize, or simply craving a nice city-caliber meal in the comfort of a unique neighborhood, saunter on by JaK's Grill. You won't be able to pass it up.

What:
JaK's Grill

Where:
4548 California Ave SW
www.jaksgrill.com
206.937.7809

When:
Monday 5–9 pm
Tuesday-Thursday 5–10 pm
Friday 4:30–11 pm
Saturday 4–11 pm
Sunday 4–9 pm

Price:
Entrées run $13.95–$49

48 | Filipino Favorites at the Manila Café

The walls are painted with deep, warm colors. The floors are finely finished. And the decorative plants are sprouting with life. In fact, the entire atmosphere feels fresh and new.

But there's something familiar about the Manila Café.

Using her grandfather Freddie's recipes, Renee Bell and her mother Sandra Martinez have recreated the famous Filipino menu that has been a favorite in Seattle for nearly half a century.

"My grandfather came to this county in 1925 at age 15. He put himself through college at the UW, served in WWII, worked at Boeing and then started a successful restaurant he ran for 47 years," beams Bell.

Also called the Manila Café back in the day, Freddie's original business began in the city's International District. Possibly one of the first of its kind in the area, this hot spot was open 24 hours a day. He later moved to a location on Delridge Way. The move was featured in a 1996 issue of the *West Seattle Herald,* as you'll see framed and displayed on the wall when you walk in the door. And now, his family is continuing his cooking tradition on the south end of California Avenue.

And the staff is no stranger to the business, either.

> **"I've been working at my grandfather's restaurant since I was 11."**
>
> Renee Bell
> co-owner

"I've been working at my grandfather's restaurant since I was 11," smiles Bell.

And when it comes to ordering the popular inihaw beef (one of Freddie's specialties), the customers know what they're doing, too.

Another crowd favorite is the adobo—a marinade of vinegar, soy sauce, and spices served on chicken or pork. In fact, people love the paprika-garlic flavor so much, they will even order a side of adobo gravy to be drizzled over a single scoop of rice.

"They also love the fried chicken," says Bell. "My grandfather made his own special recipe without batter. It's delicious."

Other menu items include pancit (Filipino sautéed noodles), garlic spareribs, and lumpia (the yummy Filipino version of egg rolls).

And don't forget to top it off with tarun—a pastry-wrapped plantain dessert sprinkled with powdered sugar (be sure to ask for the dessert specials as they change daily). The restaurant also offers lunch and breakfast on weekends.

Whether you're new to the area or a Westside veteran, you'll find a true taste of tradition at the Manila Café—where legendary Filipino flavors live on.

What:
Manila Café

Where:
6400 California Ave SW
206.932.7200

When:
Monday–Friday 11:30 am–9 pm
Saturday 9 am–9 pm
Sunday 9 am–noon

Price:
Entrées $7.95-$12.95

49 | Tea Time in the Junction

Something's steeping in the heart of the Junction. It's tea time!

Welcome to a different type of brew at Coffee to a Tea with Sugar, the neighborhood's first teahouse. Located next to West 5 Lounge, this sippers' sanctuary does offer coffee. "We have to, we're in Seattle," smiles co-owner Shanon Jensen. But its special draw is homemade baked goods and freshly brewed teas crafted with revolutionary beverage technology.

> *"Mango, green tea, and tea lattes are amazing—and a nice coffee alternative."*
>
> Jodi Baker
> co-owner

Owned by Jodi Baker and Shanon Jensen, Coffee to a Tea with Sugar brings the two women's passions to the table for you to enjoy. Jodi Baker is not the baker but rather the tea connoisseur. And Shanon Jensen, who is said to have always "inundated her friends with sugar," also runs a baking company called Sugar Rush—and mixes up a mean batch of cookies, cakes, and pies.

"This was all her idea," Jensen jests as she points to her business partner. "Jodi is a tea drinker and wanted to open a tea shop and I added Sugar Rush to complement the tea and coffee."

Try their chai tea latte and a slice of the carrot cheesecake, and you'll taste what she's talking about. But what makes it better than your average cup of tea and cake? Yummy desserts made with love surely don't hurt, but it's also the uniquely prepared Affinitea—a loose leaf tea brewed hot or iced with state-of-the-art espresso technology.

Officially called the Affinitea Beverage Infuser, this high-tech tea brewing machine delivers a fresh cup in 35 seconds. The West Seattle establishment is one of the first in the nation to run an Affinitea machine—in fact, they're the only place in the entire state of Washington to carry it.

"Mango, green tea, and tea lattes are amazing—and a nice coffee alternative," says Baker.

In addition to tea and cookies, the shop also features Tony's Coffee and entrées from Blue Willow Catering Company—all in an open, friendly atmosphere.

"We wanted to open a business close to home and at the same time create a bigger living room than we both have," says Baker. "People here can play games, read books, or come for club gatherings."

You'll see writers' clubs, book clubs, and a new wave of knitting fanatics, too.

"We wanted to create a place where friends could come and hang out and enjoy a few of life's little luxuries," says Jensen. "Just like our tagline says, this is a way to 'slow life down, one sweet moment at a time.'"

And with such a fast tea machine, there's a lot more time to enjoy it. So if you're up for a quick mango tea in under a minute, or you have time to relax and nibble on sour cream coffee cake, stop on by Coffee to a Tea with Sugar.

What:
Coffee to a Tea with Sugar

Where:
4541 California Ave SW
206.937.1495

When:
Monday–Saturday 8 am–10 pm
Sunday 8 am–4 pm

Prices:
A cup o' tea runs
$1.55-$3.55

Sugary pastries run $.25–$40.00 (for whole cakes)

Lunch entrées run $2.75–$7.95

50 | West Seattle Wine Tasting

Cheers! West Seattle's first boutique winery is here.

Jardin Wines offers wine tastings, food and wine-pairing dinners at area restaurants, special events, and plenty of reasons to pull up a chair, uncork, and unwind—a great alternative to the local bar scene.

Inhale the unmistakable aroma of pressed grapes and witness the brilliant purple Sangiovese stains on winemaker Craig Friedl's sweatshirt, and you'll know Jardin Wine is made right here in West Seattle.

For owners Bree and Craig Friedl, this labor of love started as a hobby.

"It all began about 10 years ago when a friend inherited some winemaking equipment," reflects Craig Friedl, otherwise known as Jardin's chief executive winemaker.

Before long, Friedl was flying down to UC Davis for viniculture courses and making his own labels.

"Then it got to a point where I was making too much wine to either drink or give away, so we decided to start Jardin." The pair made the business official in August of 2002.

> "We want to help take some of the mystery out of winemaking and make it available to anyone who is interested."
>
> Craig Friedl
> co-owner

The name Jardin, meaning garden in French and Spanish, stems from the Friedl's favorite setting for sipping.

"Whether you're in the Jardin des Tuileries in Paris or right in your own backyard in West Seattle, a garden bench is the very best place to enjoy a glass of great wine," smiles Bree.

Jardin Wine is produced in limited quantities but is growing in production each year. According to specialty winemakers, minimum quantity makes for maximum quality.

So how do they do it? One vineyard, one vintage at a time.

"You don't have to be a big winery to produce wine," Craig states.

Jardin crafts single vintage, terrior (or single vineyard) wines from some of the finest grapes in the Yakima Valley. First, the grapes are harvested and crushed at three different vineyards near Prosser. Then the fruits of this labor are trucked back to the West Seattle winery to be fermented, pressed, aged in oak barrels, and ultimately poured for you.

Experience Jardin's signature floral and fruit bouquet for yourself with the bold, robust flavors of the 2001 Merlot from Carter Vineyard, the not-too-sweet 2002 Dry Reisling, or the smooth finish of the Pleasant Vineyard 2001 Cabernet Sauvignon.

Attend a scheduled wine tasting, plan a private party, or participate in one of Jardin's wine-centric events. Ladies nights that feature wines and home entertaining tips are held monthly.

Want to learn more about how wine is made? The Freidls invite you to stop by and soak up all the knowledge you want. In fact, much of the winemaking process is fueled by volunteers in pursuit of winemaking know-how.

"We want to help take some of the mystery out of winemaking and make it available to anyone who is interested," nods Craig.

Which means you no longer need to trek to Napa Valley to get your viniculture fix. Just show up at a Jardin Wines event, and you'll be swirling and sniffing great wine, full of local flavor.

What:
Jardin Wines

Where:
www.jardinwines.com
206.933.2829

When:
See website for events

Price:
Bottles run $11–$21

51 | Cooking Up Dream Dinners

Wouldn't it be nice if you could somehow fix a healthy yet delicious home-cooked meal for your family in a fraction of the usual time for a fraction of the usual price and never have to ask 'what's for dinner tonight?'

Many might answer, "Dream on."

But those who have discovered the magic happening on the corner of 41st and Alaska would smile and answer, "Dream Dinners."

Owned by Leslie and Lewis Thomson, Dream Dinners serves the community by helping people sit down to eat together at the dinner table on an average of three times a week. Why?

> *"Dinner together at the table provides an important time to develop critical thinking, communication skills, decision making, social skills, and language."*
>
> Leslie Thomson
> co-owner

According to Leslie Thomson, research on National Merit Scholars over the past 20 years shows that one common thread connecting these bright individuals is the fact that they have eaten dinners at home with family members at least three times a week.

"Dinner together at the table provides an important time to develop critical thinking, communication skills, decision-making, social skills, and language," says Thomson.

So how does the Thomsons' business provide this invaluable service? A customer registers on the Dream Dinners website to set up a time and choose new entrées to prepare each month. Flavorful offerings include everything from marinated pork tenderloin to kung pao chicken. When you show up to the giant, fully stocked kitchen, your pre-portioned dinner ingredients and recipes are there waiting for your assembly at convenient prep stations. And when you're done packing up your ready-to-cook meals, the Dream Dinners crew cleans up after you.

Sound too good to be true?

There's more. Most customers say they are not only saving time by limiting trips to the grocery store and preparing the meals at home, but they are also saving money.

"We used to go the grocery story almost every day," say Mark Rekate and Tina Hansen of Shorewood. "Not only are we wasting less food, but now we can make about 16 meals for the two of us for just over $100. And the time it saves is incredible. We just made eight dinners in 50 minutes!"

Owner Leslie Thomson's shared experience with these customers is the reason she opened the store.

"What it allowed me to do was serve a nice, healthy, handmade dinner for the family and at the same time be more relaxed by saving time and money."

A registered dietician and diabetes nutrition specialist for the Diabetes Care Center at UW Medical Center, Thomson was no easy food critic to impress.

"I know that getting healthy meals on the table is a struggle for everyone. We all WANT to eat well at home, but so many things get in the way."

What:
Dream Dinners

Where:
4701 41st Ave SW, #110
www.dreamdinners.com
206.938.5999

When:
Check website or call
as schedule varies

Price:
Check website or call
as entrée prices change
monthly

Thomson is proud to say her business is now making a difference for all kinds of people in the community.

"It's not just for soccer moms, but everyone who wants to save time and money—empty-nesters, singles, students, you name it," she smiles. "I feel good about opening Dream Dinners because I am able to help make the people in this community happier and healthier."

Tune into local music and culture at Easy Street Records.

ARTS & ENTERTAINMENT

A veritable mecca of music and art, West Seattle offers inspiring ways to entertain both your inner child and your sophisticated side. Whether you're into markets or movies, or prefer dancing and singing, you'll find a little taste of everything in this group of 24 things to do.

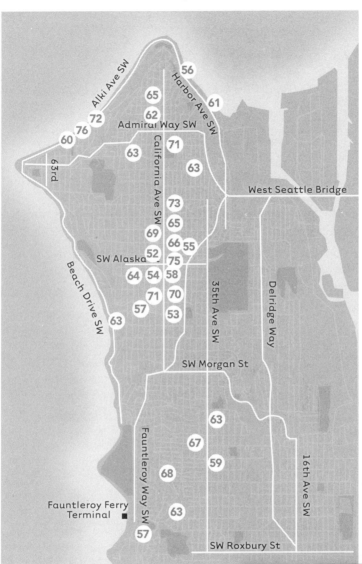

56

65

62

72

76

60

63rd

63

71

Alki Ave SW

Harbor Ave SW

61

Admiral Way SW

California Ave SW

63

73

65

69

66 55

52

75

SW Alaska

64 54 58

71 70

57

53

Beach Drive SW

63

35th Ave SW

Delridge Way

West Seattle Bridge

SW Morgan St

63

67

59

68

Fauntleroy Way SW

16th Ave SW

Fauntleroy Ferry
Terminal ▪

63

57

SW Roxbury St

52 | Tune into Local Music at Easy Street

The Hank Williams omelet. The rock-a-billy barista. And one of Seattle's best collection of tunes. Easy Street Records—a mecca for music fans—began with a West Seattle teen who was into the music scene.

Raised by a mom in the music biz and working at record stores throughout high school, owner Matt Vaughan was exposed to the industry at an early age.

"I can honestly say that throughout my teenage years, I was in a record store every day," recalls Vaughan.

Taken under his boss' wing, he had the opportunity to buy the business, and opened Easy Street in 1988.

Along the way from being the only employee originally to having several dozen today, Vaughan rode the wave of Seattle's growing music scene. He began live music in-stores, became a member of the Coalition of Independent Record Stores, started a hip diner-style café, and opened a second location on Queen Anne. And though a lot has happened in the past couple decades, not much has changed.

> "In my earlier years, a common day would be to meet friends at a record store and then go to the IHOP and sit there for hours having coffee, talking about music and girls."
>
> Matt Vaughan
> owner

"In my earlier years," he reflects, "a common day would be to meet friends at a record store and then go to the IHOP and sit there for hours having coffee, talking about music and girls."

Now, Vaughan owns the record store and the IHOP (so to speak) in his favorite 'hood. And he wouldn't have it any other way. Nor would

ARTS & ENTERTAINMENT

the loyal music listeners that line the bar stools in search of new tunes each day.

You can sample music while you sip your latte at listening stations, an activity otherwise known as "Easy Listening." Every month the music-savvy staff prepares a fresh mix of CDs for you to taste-test.

With eclectic selections ranging from Joe Strummer to Willie Nelson and Supergrass, Easy Listening has something for everyone.

"It's an easy way for people to listen to new music," says store manager Adam Tutty. "You can sit back, relax, have some eggs, and get turned on to something new at the same time."

If you like what you hear, it just so happens that the selections are on special for a 2-month period until the next wave begins.

So whether you're looking for new music to add to your collection or simply want to toe-tap while sipping your double tall, tune into the local scene at Easy Street Records and turn onto a neighborhood tradition.

What:
Easy Street Records

Where:
4559 California Ave SW
www.EasyStreetOnline.com
206.938.EASY

When:
Monday–Saturday 9 am–9 pm
Sunday 11 am–7 pm

The café is open
7 am–3 pm daily

Price:
Entrées run $3.95–$8.25

53 | Sip & Sway at C & P

Something's brewing in the 100-year-old Craftsman on California. Sure, you can smell the aroma of Lighthouse Roasters fine espresso from the sidewalk and see the word "coffee" on the sign, but step inside and you'll discover a whole lot more.

C & P Coffee—a true neighborhood coffeehouse with a cozy fireplace—is home to some of the city's best beans, as well as a growing community of local artists and musicians.

> "The caliber of musicians who play here is incredible, and the most fascinating thing about it is that they are our neighbors."
>
> Cameron Moores
> co-owner

"It's really organic how it all came together," beams Cameron Moores who owns the coffeehouse with her husband Pete (hence the "C & P" name). "Once we opened, local artists and musicians just started coming in the door, offering to play and share their talents with West Seattle."

A coffee connoisseur, Moores has been in the business of brewing a great cup for over 14 years. So coffee has always been the main focus at C & P. But she's been pleasantly surprised with what else the community has brought to her business.

"The caliber of musicians who play here is incredible," she smiles. "And the most fascinating thing about it is that they are our neighbors. We're so lucky to be surrounded with so many talented people."

Every Saturday Marco de Carvalho performs with a different combination of professional jazz musicians. The word has spread to the Brazilian community, and now entire Brazilian families flock to this weekly Latin treat.

"Bands really enjoy this venue because they can bring their families," explains Moores. "They are used to playing late-night in smoky bars, and this provides a warm, inviting environment for them."

In addition to jazz, the coffeehouse venue also features bluegrass, acoustic guitar, spoken word, poetry readings, and a monthly art show.

Besides serving up coffee and entertainment, the ultimate goal of C&P is to become a community space. The coffeehouse hosts political meetings as well as voter registration and has been a gathering place in the neighborhood for many, many years.

"Once a 95-year-old woman came in here and told me that she came to this house for a 'fancy dress' ball," says Moores. "People really like the feel of this place, and neat things happen here. We've had two authors finish their books here, toddlers have learned to walk here, and political figures make important decisions here."

Offering free wireless Internet access alongside the age-old tradition of gathering around a cup of coffee with community members, you could say that C&P is progressive while embracing the family values of the past.

"There's a new energy in West Seattle—young families, artists, political activists—an undercurrent of people for positive growth in the community," explains Moores. "We hope to be a part of that spirit."

So if you'd like to catch the community wave—while sitting by the fire, sampling some of the city's best coffee and listening to live local tunes in the comfort of an historic Westside home—come sip & sway at C & P.

What:
C & P Coffee Company

Where:
5612 California Ave SW
www.candpcoffee.com
206.933.3125

When:
Monday–Friday 6:30 am–8 pm
Saturday & Sunday 7 am–8 pm

Price:
Coffee prices vary depending on your personal taste; inquire within

54 | Late Night Laughs with Improv

Looking for a night out on the town but want to stay in the neighborhood? Come for the fun at ArtsWest Playhouse. On select Saturday nights, ArtsWest hosts West Seattle's own Late Nite improvisational comedy.

Making sides hurt (in a good way) since 2001, improv groups bring a welcome Late Nite addition to the West Seattle scene.

"There's nothing else like it in the neighborhood," says ArtsWest director Michael Harris. "In addition to all the plays and musical events we do here, this is a fun way for people to spend a weekend night out."

You can almost feel the humor in the air as showtime approaches, but the hilarity doesn't officially begin until 10:00 p.m. The schedule rotates to feature a wide range of local sensations. Some past performances have included groups such as Jet City Improv, the Sisters of Sal, Lipshtick, Improv Faction, and Scatterbrains Improv (to name a few), and the list of laughs goes on.

"We rotate groups on a weekly basis to keep the audience freshly entertained each time they come," says marketing manager Carlene Canton.

Still, even with the same group, no two shows are the same, so sampling several Saturdays is recommended. Most shows feature lots of audience participation in the form of games, sketches, and musical numbers—based entirely on suggestions from the crowd. Filled with quick wit and impromptu, off-the-cuff humor, the show ensures a new experience each time.

> *You can almost feel the humor in the air as showtime approaches, but the hilarity doesn't officially begins until 10:00 p.m.*

But Late Nite at ArtsWest doesn't stop with improv. The venue also features

ARTS & ENTERTAINMENT

singer showcases, stand-up comics, novelty acts, live bands, dance, and performance art.

And if Late Nite entertainment doesn't suit you, maybe the myriad of ArtsWest's other offerings will. The community playhouse is best known for its award-winning theater and also features art exhibits, concerts, and arts-related education programs like summer youth theater.

"We're here to create the kind of art that reflects ourselves to ourselves—a great way to grow as individuals and as a community," says director Michael Harris. "And our youth work is key to developing artists and audiences for the future."

From a mid-life late-nighter to a middle school teen, any West Seattleite can truly connect to the community theater.

"We are committed to art that involves and inspires people of all ages and backgrounds," Harris conculudes. "It's as essential as food, water, and air!"

So, if you need a good laugh come the weekend or you simply want to experience the arts in a friendly neighborhood atmosphere, enter ArtsWest, hold on to your seat, and prepare to be entertained.

What:
Late Nite Improv
(and more)

Where:
ArtsWest Playhouse
4711 California Ave SW
www.artswest.com
206.938.0339

When:
See website for monthly listings

Price:
Improv tickets run
$5–$7; see website
for other events

55 | Glow Zone at West Seattle Bowl

It's an average Saturday night. You walk into a familiar place. Then you notice that the lights shine black and your teeth gleam green. A disco ball turns and the DJ spins his first tune. A new bar? No. A dance club? Uh-uh. It's West Seattle Bowl's one and only Glow Zone.

> *Come early if you want the neon pink and yellow bowling shoes, though—the ones that glow tend to go first.*

Every Saturday night West Seattleites and visitors from afar (such as Ballard) gather from 11 p.m. to 1 a.m. to get funky to the sound of pins dropping as they bowl the night away.

Featuring a wide range of music, from classic rock and pop to '80s and before, along with club-style lighting, the Glow Zone offers you a chance to go out without going downtown.

For one price, you and your friends can rent shoes, listen to tunes, and bowl as many games as you can squeeze into two and a half hours. Depending on the number in your party and your personal strike-ability, this can amount to quite an evening-ful. If you're hungry, you can grab a late night bite from the Chinese restaurant attached to the bowling center. And since this sport works up a mean thirst, there's a bar behind lane 15 (just don't bring your pitchers of beer down to the finely waxed floor, or, well, accidents can happen).

Manager Andy Carl says that West Seattle Bowl started the Glow Zone when "cosmic bowling" began to take off throughout the U.S. "We opened the Glow Zone on January 10, 1999, and it's been going strong ever since."

The Glow Zone runs all year long, but winter months gather the biggest crowds. "Usually January through May are our busiest months," says long-time Glow Zone worker Brian Mueller.

Mueller can't count the number of shoes he goes through on a jammin'

February night, but there always seem to be enough for glow bowlers to share. Come early if you want the neon pink and yellow bowling shoes, though—the ones that glow tend to go first.

Want to share glow-in-the-dark fun with a crowd of friends? You can also rent a lane (or ten) and host a Glow Zone party for birthdays, work events, or any other excuse you've got. There are three different packages to choose from so you can customize or create a theme for your event.

So don't forget to practice your form in the mirror on Friday nights. When it comes to Saturdays, you'll be in the zone.

What:
Glow Bowling

Where:
West Seattle Bowl
4505 39th Ave SW
www.wsbowl.com
206.932.3731

When:
Saturday from 11 pm–1 am
(Check-in begins at 10 pm)

Price:
$12.00 pre–paid before 6 pm
$14.00 on–site

Or, $55.00 per lane (for up to 6 people)

Note: There is a $5.00 cover for anyone not bowling

Kids awaiting instruction at Lee's Martial Arts parent-child tae kwon do class

Alki Kayak Tour's
brightly colored crafts

Bus and coffee stop in the heart of the West Seattle Junction

Alki Bathhouse Art Studio

Local art depicting Ray Charles adorns
diner walls at Easy Street Records

Avalon Glass artist Ryan Kells cooks up a toasty batch of blown glass while cool, finished pieces glow in the gallery (below)

Taps a plenty poised to pour pints while traditional signage draws in pub-goers at Celtic Swell Irish Pub on Alki (below)

Fauntleroy ferry and a flotilla of anchored
sailboats off the shores of Lincoln Park

West Seattle ice cream icon Husky Deli

A steaming cup of joe amidst strumming guitar music and classic espresso signage at C & P Coffee Co.

Mother's Day poppies at the Farmers Market

Espresso

Copper salmon sculpture by Lee Emmons at
Salty's on Alki gets ready to swallow up Seattle

Locals and visitors alike ride the Alki Beach boardwalk on classic Del Sol beach cruisers for hire at Coastal Surf Boutique

See what you can find—from wildlife to container ship cargo—with eye-opening viewfinders on Alki Beach

"Midnight Call" historical mural by Don Barrie depicts a horse-drawn fire rig at the original Junction Station location

The Murals of WEST SEATTLE

"Midnight Call" #323

The horse-drawn hose Company #323 responds feverishly to a fire call in the wee hours of a 1914 night. Fire Station #32 was built in 1914 on the southeast corner of 44th and Alaska St (across the street) and opened with one hosewagon and two gray horses. In 1917, the city added a police station manning the post with one motorcycle officer. The building served the community for fifty years as a fire station and police precinct and public restrooms. In 1970, services moved to modern quarters picturesque old building was razed to become a parking lot.

Dedicated Nov. 1990
Major Funding: Don Swanson, Seattle
K.C. Centennial Commission

No 3

Local pooch awaiting his owner on Junction corner

CAFE
OPEN 7 A.M.
7 Days a Week

COFFEE BA

yoga

"Flaming" Bikram Yoga building

Classic signage at local cocktail lounge

FRESH
CHIVES
$1.50 BUNCH

FRESH
THYME
$1.50 BUNCH

FRESH
MINT
$1.50 BU!

Fresh herbs and produce at the
Sunday Farmers Market

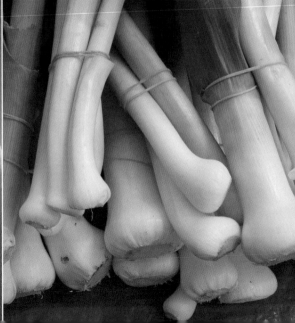

Robe awaiting a spa-goer
at Head-to-Toe Day Spa

A West Seattleite's view of the big city from the pi... at Seacrest Marina

Luna Park neighborhood sign welcomes residents and visitors to West Seattle

West Seattle "inbox"

Westside seagulls soar over Puget Sour

A spot to rest at C & P Coffee Co.

Sign affirming what motorists have already noticed

A pint of handcrafted Alembic Pale Ale and barstools on which to sip it at Elliott Bay Brewery

SCENIC DRIVE 4

Lady Liberty stands proud on the shores of Alki Beach marking the birthplace of Seattle

Alki Kayak Tour's guide Greg
Whittaker paddles in Puget Sound

56 | Blues Night at Alki Tavern

When you hear the extra loud hum of Harleys, you know it's Thursday night and hoards of bikers are heading down the strip to Alki Tavern. And if you ride, Taco Thursdays are a thunderous tradition, similar to something you might see in So-Cal.

But on the weekend Alki Tavern also offers another, slightly subtler sound that few neighborhood bars can rival: the blues.

On Sunday nights from 5 p.m.– 9 p.m., some of the best blues acts in town flock to the bar (otherwise known for its bikers) for some serious playing. From Chicago blues to Delta blues and even a taste of New Orleans, Alki Tavern offers a broad range in a genre that's attracting more than the typical crowd.

With show-goers ranging in age from 21 to 81, Blues Night brings in a wide variety of music fans from across the city to enjoy great tunes with a scenic backdrop. Many appreciate the atmosphere—it's lively enough for dancing, yet mellow enough for conversation or a game of pool. Another Blues Night bonus is simply the timeframe.

> *"The greatest blues players in town will play here because they know it's one of the best gigs in town. It's hard to beat blues on the beach, and this is one of the most unique watering holes you'll find."*
>
> Marlee Walker
> editor of "Blues to Do"

"It's early enough on Sunday night that you can go out and hear some great music but still be in shape for work the next day," says organizer and schoolteacher Cathy McLynne. "Sunday Blues Night is a good way to end one week or a great way to start off the next."

McLynne, whose husband Gill has run the tavern for more than a quarter of a century, began Blues Night in 2001. "It's her baby," smiles Gill.

"We used to have live music here for things like Christmas parties but really wanted to start something weekly," reflects Cathy. "And we were inspired by our love of the blues."

So began Blues Night with help from Marlee Walker, blues enthusiast and editor of "Blues to Do," a blues newsletter and online source for blues happenings around town.

"It's been a real hoot," says Walker. "It's the longest-running weekly blues night in the area, and the atmosphere is great. You really get a wide cross section of West Seattle blues fans, from your regulars to yuppies, hippies, and retirees on Harleys. It's entertaining."

And according to Walker, Alki Tavern is a sought-after venue for top musicians.

"The greatest blues players in town will play here because they know it's one of the best gigs in town," she explains. "It's hard to beat blues on the beach, and this is one of the most unique watering holes you'll find."

So if you're thinking about giving Alki Tavern a try, don't worry if you don't own a pair of chaps. On sun-setting Sunday nights, there's no better place to be for beach views, a beer, and the blues.

What:
Sunday Blues Night

Where:
Alki Tavern
1321 Harbor Ave SW
www.bluestodo.com
206.932.9970

When:
Sunday 5–9 pm

Price:
No cover

57 | Stay & Play at Westside B&Bs

Whether you have relatives coming into town or you need to "get away" for a night yourself, put West Seattle's bed and breakfasts on your list of "101 things to do."

"I've even had people come and stay from as close as across the street," says Judy Burbrink, owner of Villa Heidelberg B&B. "Sure, we have a lot of guests visiting from out of town, but many people right here in the neighborhood come to stay for birthdays, anniversaries, or just a special night away."

> *"I've even had people come and stay from as close as across the street!"*
>
> Judy Burbrink
> owner of Villa Heidelberg B&B

West Seattle offers two B&B options, one on each end of town.

Villa Heidelberg

A home and garden with European roots, Villa Heidelberg B&B was built in 1909 by Jacob Mades of Heidelberg, Germany. Currently owned and operated by Judy Burbrink, the B&B is also home to her life-long European dream.

"After staying in bed and breakfasts in Europe, I always wanted to open one," she reflects.

Located just steps from the Junction in the heart of West Seattle, Villa Heidelberg is in walking distance of restaurants like JaK's Grill and Mashiko Sushi as well as the Elliott Bay Brewery and ArtsWest Playhouse—perfect for a night out on the town.

The house itself has six guestrooms themed after German towns. Features include classic beamed ceilings, original Mission light fixtures, leaded glass windows, a fireplace, and a wraparound porch with views of Puget Sound and the Olympics.

But the bed is just part of the experience. Don't forget the breakfast!

"I serve a full, hot breakfast every day," says Burbrink. "And I vary the china as well as the menu for those staying multiple days."

Breakfast can range from hotcakes to the signature Northwest Eggs Benedict with asparagus and smoked salmon to blueberry French toast.

Wildwood B&B

Straight out of the Cotswolds—but in West Seattle's Fauntleroy neighborhood—is Wildwood Bed and Breakfast. A cottage-like home and garden with old English elegance, this five-room B&B has frequently been likened to "taking a step back in time."

"The home was designed by an architect for his wife in 1923," says owner Linda Carol Keith. "With details such as built-in nooks and crannies, a lovely open staircase, and antiques, it brings back memories of a simpler time."

What:
Westside B&Bs

Where:
Villa Heidelberg B&B
4845 45th Avenue SW
www.villaheidelberg.com
206.938.3658

Wildwood B&B
4518 SW Wildwood Place
www.wildwoodseattle.com
206.819.9075

When:
Year-round

Price:
(including full breakfasts)

Villa Heidelberg B&B
$90–$150 per night

Wildwood B&B
$70–$115 per night

Wildwood guests enjoy the area's surroundings—it's convenient (on the bus line and close to the airport); it's beautiful (just steps from Lincoln Park and scenic ferry rides); and, on top of the big breakfast served on fine English bone china, there's lunch and dinner available across the street at Endolyne Joe's.

So whether you choose to stay in Wildwood's romantic Victorian or Tudor Room with garden views, idyllic surroundings will make tourists want to go out and play while West Seattleites will feel as if they've arrived at country cottage somewhere in jolly old England.

58 | Get Down with DJ Kirk Dubb

Want to boogie down? Take a detour from downtown and don your dancing shoes for DJ night at the Rocksport. Every Friday night from 10 p.m. till close DJ Kirk Dubb will be spinning the best of many music genres—disco, rock, dance, hip hop, funk—and undoubtedly lots of surprises.

"I'll do whatever it takes to get the Rocksporters' dancing shoes groovin' and keep the party going," nods DJ Kirk Dubb. "Everyone likes to hear good music when they're out on a Friday night."

And he's got the goods to back it up.

"I've been digging for records since about 1990," remarks DJ Kirk Dubb. "I have a couple thousand records in my collection."

A local talent who also frequents the establishment as a customer, DJ Kirk Dubb knows the biz as well as the clientele.

"DJ Kirk Dubb has a good knowledge of music in general and knows what people like to listen to," explains Rocksport owner Dan Beeman. "He pulls out some of that old school funk that everyone really likes. He has an eclectic ear."

The first act of its kind for the venue, DJ night is just what his customers ordered, says Beeman.

> *"Everyone likes to hear good music when they're out on a Friday night."*
>
> DJ Kirk Dubb

"Now, instead of large groups heading downtown to the dance clubs to see live DJs, they are dancing in their own neighborhood," says Beeman. "We have big sound, quality equipment, disco lights, and the best DJ in the West."

"It's a fun place to hang out and party on a Friday night," says the mixmaster himself.

"DJ Kirk Dubb gives West Seattle what we want," smiles Beeman.

And the best part? No cover. DJ night also coincides with "drink promo nights," so plenty of giveaways and drink specials are available as well—making it an affordable spot to dance your Friday night away.

And because boogying down can work up an appetite, the Rocksport also offers a full menu until 10 p.m. with appetizers and pizza available all night long. Now that's a party.

What:
Dancing to DJ Kirk Dubb

Where:
The Rocksport
4209 SW Alaska Street
www.rocksport.net
206.935.5838

When:
Friday nights
10 pm–close (approx. 1:30 am)

Price:
Gratis

59 | Vintage Vaudeville at Kenyon Hall

Looking for something different to do this weekend? Head for Kenyon Hall.

"One of the Seven Wonders of West Seattle," according to an anonymous source, Kenyon Hall features an eclectic array of entertainment from vaudeville shows to silent movies accompanied by a 1929 Wurlitzer pipe organ. You'll also find magic shows, comedy acts, and musical performances featuring local, national, and international entertainers.

> *"It's a place to bring your parents and a place to bring your kids. And it's a way for people in the artistic community to reach out to West Seattleites in an intimate setting."*
>
> Lou Magor
> Kenyon Hall founder

"It's a place to bring your parents and a place to bring your kids," says founder Lou Magor. "And it's a way for people in the artistic community to reach out to West Seattleites in an intimate setting."

Kenyon Hall came to be in 1993 as Hokum Hall.

"My colleagues and I wanted a place to perform," reflects Magor. "This hall was a true find, with an established tradition of holding community gatherings."

So a handful of performers, with a cumulative background in music, theater, radio, and entertainment, began sharing their talents with the neighborhood. And more than a decade later, they're still deep in the heart of vaudeville.

What exactly is vaudeville? It can be anything from a short satirical song to a full-blown variety show. The term originated from the French "chanson du Vau de Vire," a song from a region in Normandy.

Though they do their part to splash the neighborhood with classic culture, Kenyon Hall's founders say they do have other "day jobs." But Magor assures that "this is where our real interest lies."

And their interest appeals to all ages, making Kenyon Hall an inexpensive option for families who like to go out without leaving West Seattle.

"Families can experience history here," exclaims Magor. "We want to give young people the chance to spend a weekend night seeing and hearing a type of entertainment from the past that simply does not exist anywhere else."

But Kenyon Hall is not just about nighttime theater.

"During the day, we're developing little musicians through our Kindermusik program," says Magor. Kindermusik is an early childhood education program for children ages newborn to seven. It helps kids and their families learn more about music.

In addition to the weekend performances and music classes, Kenyon Hall can also be rented out for parties, weddings, and more.

"We did a wedding here that included the ceremony and reception, and afterward, we turned out the lights and watched a silent movie about Buster Keaton building a dream house after getting married. It was wonderful."

According to Magor, Kenyon Hall appreciates creativity and will do what it can to encourage and accommodate out-of-the-ordinary requests. But just walking through the front door you know you're about to be part of something unique. No wonder it's a Wonder.

What:
Variety Shows at Kenyon Hall

Where:
7904 35th Ave SW
www.kenyonhall.org
206.937.3613

When:
Visit the website for an events calendar

Price:
Live shows run $14 for reserved table seats, $12 for row seats (senior/student $10)

Sunday Family Matinees are $8 per person or $25 per family

60 | Art at Alki Bathhouse

Be a part of art right here in West Seattle at Alki Bathhouse. For years the Bathhouse has drawn students and artists who enjoy a creative outlet at the inspiring beachfront setting.

And now, thanks to funds from the Pro Parks Levy, Alki Community Center Advisory Council, Friends of the Bathhouse, and the Seattle Department of Neighborhoods, Alki Bathhouse offers even more in its rebuilt, multipurpose facility, full of color inside and out.

Aptly named, the Bathhouse was part of Alki's thriving summer swim scene decades ago. Just yards off shore, kids and vacationers alike would pile on floating rafts, jumping and diving into the chilly Sound and hopping back out to warm up in the sun. Draft horses arrived each fall to take the rafts away until the next season, and finally, in the 1950s, the rafts were removed for good.

But, happily, the beach still remains a gathering place for folks who want to have fun.

Trading in old-fashioned swimsuits for modern-day painters' smocks, the Alki Bathhouse of today is home to budding artists of all ages and a "practice facility" for the pros. Classes for all levels are held for kids and adults while studio space is open for seasoned veterans.

> Trading in old-fashioned swimsuits for modern-day painters' smocks, the Alki Bathhouse of today is home to budding artists of all ages and a "practice facility" for the pros.

The classes vary each season, offering everything from cartooning to basketry to filmmaking to summer art camp. Some of the art studio's returning favorites are drawing, watercolor painting, pottery, and wheel throwing.

All Bathhouse activities are organized and operated

by community staff at the Alki Community Center.

"The Bathhouse is a tremendous asset for the community center and for the neighborhood," says Alki Community Center recreation coordinator John Hermann. "It offers affordable yet high-quality programs as well as a space for trained artists to create."

So whether you're a beginner or an expert, the Bathhouse offers a time and a place to discover your personal creativity while focusing on unwinding and escaping the worries of daily life—all in a highly constructive way. Sure, making art and taking classes are great social activities, but they're also effective ways to relieve stress—channeling the good through colors, shapes, lines, and textures.

After all, even if you love creating art, it's easy to let other things get in the way when you don't consciously make time for it. With a class in place, it's almost like insurance that you will make the effort to do what you love. Many Bathhouse artists go regularly for this very reason—a sacred window of time and space to do nothing but create.

So whether you are artistically challenged and only draw stick figures or you have years of dried paint layered on your favorite art apron, try diving into the Bathhouse for artistic inspiration, Alki-style.

What:
Art Classes & Studios

Where:
Alki Bathhouse
2701 Alki Ave SW
www.seattle.gov/parks/
Arts/alkiart.htm
206.684.7430

When:
Stop by the studio for a brochure or see website for class schedules

Price:
See printed or online brochure

61 | *Cruise to Mariner Games via Water Taxi*

It's a sunny Saturday. Elliott Bay glimmers like an invitation to get wet. The smell of beach barbeques and the salty sea breeze is rivaled only by the baseball fever in the air. But you don't have to choose between splashing around in the Sound and America's favorite pastime—you can have both.

Get your Mojo minus the traffic hassles of Sodo—all without spending mucho.

Thanks to the Elliott Bay Water Taxi, baseball fans (and boating fans) can be whisked across the bay for a day of peanuts and Crackerjacks—and catch a few waves to and fro. Mariner season (throughout spring and summertime) is prime time for getting out on the water and catching a fly ball while you're at it.

A great day out on the Bay and at Safeco Field provides a perfect activity to share with out-of-town visitors or friends and family right from the shores of West Seattle. Just pick the game you want to see, match it up with a suitable Water Taxi time, and you're set. No driving necessary, no outrageous parking fees. Total time on the water runs only about 12 minutes.

In other words, you can get your Mojo minus the traffic hassles of Sodo—all without spending mucho.

In fact, the Water Taxi offers dedicated sailings just to accommodate Mariner fans after the game so you don't have to leave before the ninth inning in order to get home. For weekday games, it operates on the extended "Friday" schedule, and on weekends the extension is already built in. But don't dally—it's still a bit of a walk or a cab ride from Safeco Field to Pier 55. As long as you're conscious of the time, you should be fine.

On weekends the Water Taxi runs every hour on the hour from 9 a.m.–7 p.m., and until 11 p.m. on Saturdays. Weekday sailings are a bit sporadic, and the schedule changes from year to year, so always check the website for current schedules or pick up a brochure at Seacrest Marina.

So for a fun way to arrive at even more fun, consider taking the taxi that floats. They are the "Mariners," after all—wouldn't they be proud to have West Seattle travel by boat to see them sink their opponents?

And even if baseball isn't your game, taking the Water Taxi is great for a day at the Pike Place Market, the Seattle Aquarium, or a walk along the downtown waterfront.

What:
Elliott Bay Water Taxi

Where:
Seacrest Marina to Pier 55
1660 Harbor Ave SW
http://transit.metrokc.gov
206.684.2046

www.mariners.org

When:
Spring & summer (sailing schedules vary yearly; please see website for current times)

Price:
$3 one way (age 5 and under are free), plus your Mariners ticket

62 | Dinner and a Movie in Admiral

If you're tired of TV and the impersonality of megaplexes has got you down, look to a friendly neighborhood on the north side. West Seattleites and visitors alike can take in dinner and a movie at the historic Admiral Theater—all for under $20 per person.

Depending on whether you're a matinee-goer or a late-night lounger, you can visit nearby restaurants before or after your flick for innovative pub food, a taste of Thai, or fresh-baked bagel sandwiches—just look within a block of the Admiral.

Admiral Theatre

The historic West Seattle cinema was originally built as the live-stage Portolo Acting Theater and opened in 1919. Numerous decades and several owners later, the renamed Admiral Theater features two 400-person auditoriums with antique theater seats and modernday movies. The lobby has a salty cruise motif complete with theater designations of "Port 1" and "Port 2." Concessions run about half the price of your average theater, and movie tickets are just $4.50.

Though it harkens back to days of old, the Admiral Theater features recent flicks as well as the infamous cult classic *The Rocky Horror Picture Show* on the first Saturday of the month at midnight. If you happen to walk by the theater before showtime on a *Rocky Horror* night, you're bound to see a show outside as well. People go all-out for this event, from fishnets to full patent leather ensembles, all while chanting, "Let's do the time warp agaaaaain."

> *Admiral Theater features two 400-person auditoriums with antique theater seats and modern-day movies.*

Circa Neighborhood Grill & Alehouse

One intersection and a few steps south of the theater is Circa Neighborhood Grill & Alehouse. This friendly little bistro caters to the movie crowd, but be sure to come early, as seating is limited.

The menu fits the tagline, "Creative Comfort Food," and, of course, typical pub grub is available; it is an alehouse after all. You can also feast on grilled skirt-steak, pork loin, or jerk chicken along with your domestic microbrew or import, if you wish.

Pailin Thai

Pailin lies just north of the theater and is often packed with loyal customers, movie-goers, and take-out artists. But a full house is a good sign and they always seem to be able to squeeze you in anyway. Spring rolls dipped in plum sauce are a tasty appetizer, and for only about $7 you can feast on any number of traditional Thai entrées including panang beef, pad thai, or swimming rama with tasty peanut sauce.

Zatz A Better Bagel

Directly across the street from the theater is Zatz A Better Bagel. These fresh-baked treats are great to eat any time of day. Try an egg and bagel sandwich for a late breakfast before a midday matinee, or pile up a pesto bagel with deli meats and vegetables for lunch. And if you don't have much time to stop and eat before the show, Zatz's bagel dogs are good to go.

How often does a full night of entertainment cost less than a Jackson? Easy—every night you hit the Admiral and it's fleet of surrounding restaurants.

What:
Dinner and a Movie

Where:
Admiral Theater
2343 California Ave SW
www.admiral-theater.com
206.938.3456

Circa Grill & Alehouse
2605 California Ave SW
206.923.1102

Pailin Thai
2223 California Ave SW
206.937.8807

Zatz A Better Bagel
2348 California Ave SW
206.933.8244

When:
Check the website or call for showtimes

Price:
Movies are $4.50
Rocky Horror is $5
Restaurants vary

63 | Cruisin' for Christmas Lights

This holiday season, take the time to escape your present-wrapping frenzy and go cruisin' for Christmas lights. It's a great way to explore unfamiliar nooks and crannies in West Seattle and when you find the well-lit Yuletide treasures, it feels like you've found the prize.

At this time of year, it doesn't matter whose lawn is greener, but whose inflatable lawn art is bigger.

The neighborhood's best and brightest can be seen many ways: by foot (if you want to stay close to home); by bike (if you want to catch the views in a couple of hoods and get some exercise at the same time); or by car (if quick trips, lots of coverage, and keeping warm are top notches on your list).

At this time of year, it doesn't matter whose lawn is greener, but whose inflatable lawn art is bigger and whose lights shine brighter in the dark winter sky. Nothing's wrong with a little friendly neighborhood competition, especially when it's helping spread the spirit.

Some neighborhoods even plan parties around the brightly-lit spectacles for a fun break in the evening and an excuse to fill travel mugs with toasty beverages and wander down the street.

But make sure you hit the streets before too late, because many follow the "lights out before bed" philosophy and shut their operations down early. Best viewing times are generally between 6 p.m. and 10 p.m.

Every neighborhood has its favorites, but here are few that seem to shine year after year.

The Menashe Family "Winter Wonderland"
Cruise along Beach Drive between Lincoln Park and Alki in December and you can't help but notice the shimmering holiday estate that seems to grow brighter each year. At 5605 Beach Drive, you'll see scores of Santas, reindeer frolicking on the roof and in the yard, carolers, a larger-

than-life toy soldier, an abominable snowman, and signs that direct you to the North Pole (in case you were wondering which way to go).

Fauntlee Hills "Candy Cane Lane"
Follow Barton to 41st, go north to SW Concord, and witness a winding row of decked-out holiday homes. From gingerbread men and shining stars to giant snowman and a Santa-shaped hedge, this street has all sorts of holiday cheer in one brightly lit block.

Fire Station "Light Fest"
On 35th and Othello, the sirens are not the only things glowing in the holiday season. The fire station does its part to light up the neighborhood, without smoke or flame.

Belvidere "Bliss"
A merry home on the corner of Hinds and Belvidere offers residents a one-stop glimpse at a line-up of glowing orange luminaries, a virtual "Candy Cane Lane," and a hint of the tropics with lit-up palm trees.

South Admiral "Pole"
Swing by 45th and Stevens for Santa and his reindeer perched on the rooftop, a myriad of lights, and generally good all-around glow.

What:
Cruisin' for Christmas Lights

Where:
Beach Drive
Fauntlee Hills
35th Ave and Othello
Belvidere and Hinds
South Admiral

When:
Approx 6–10 pm nightly from early December through the holidays

Price:
Free if you walk or bike, or the price of gas to get there

64 | Get Fresh at Farmers Market

Bring on the broccolini and wild seasonal greens. Like a welcoming spring flower, the West Seattle Farmers Market returns to the heart of the neighborhood each May.

A little taste of country in the city, the Farmers Market features a family-friendly place to go for fresh produce and casual conversation with the very farmers who grow the goods. You'll find a wide variety of products from more than 35 Washington State farmers for sale every week.

Nibble on samples of fresh cherries or berries, grab a fresh-cut mum for mom, and see produce evolve into tempting dishes at the on-site cooking demos.Threre's also live music and activities for kids.

Open on Sundays from 10 a.m. till 2 p.m., May through December, the West Seattle Farmers Market is located in the Alaska Junction at the corner of SW Alaska and California Avenue. Look for the parking lot just behind the bus shelters on Alaska.

Once the market is up and running for the season, fresh sheets listing the bounty of the week's harvest are posted on the website so you can do meal-planning before you arrive. There's even an option to receive a weekly email fresh sheet to remind you. But feel free to be tempted with a spontaneous cinnamon roll or batch of fresh pasta, too.

> *Nibble on samples of fresh cherries or berries, grab a fresh-cut mum for mom, and see produce evolve into tempting dishes at the on-site cooking demos.*

Operating since 1999, the market is referred to by locals as West Seattle's "newest best tradition." Besides providing fresh, healthy foods and a fun Sunday pastime, the Farmers Market also gives back to the community by encouraging shoppers to explore the surrounding retail businesses and area restaurants. Wander across the street to sample CDs at the independent record store Easy Street or walk up to window-shop at Menashe & Sons Jewelry for a kind of karat you won't see for sale at the market.

The market is also certified to accept electronic food stamps and WIC Farmers Market Nutrition Program Coupons. And, at closing time, farmers donate leftover produce to neighborhood food banks—totaling thousands of pounds by season's end.

The direct-sale of these Washington farmers' produce also helps retain their livelihood. In fact, the Seattle area farmers markets provide a living wage for more than 140 of our region's small farmers.

All this means that you can really feel good about getting fresh at the Farmers Market each Sunday—fresh produce, that is.

What:
West Seattle Farmers Market

Where:
Junction of Alaska
and California Ave
www.seattlefarmersmarkets.org

When:
Sundays 10 am–2 pm
May–Dec. (check back annually
for specific dates)

Price:
Free to see, but bring some
green if you want to buy greens

65 | Go Antiquing

Want to try something old this weekend? A way of life to fanatics or a perfect pastime for newcomers, searching for antiques and collectibles in West Seattle is a great way to appreciate yesterday today.

Start in the heart of the West Seattle Junction at the Antique Mall (in the old JC Penney's building) and head to North Admiral to Admiralty House Antiques for specialty items and collectibles.

> *"The great thing about collectors is that they are holding onto pieces of our history for us."*
>
> Jenny Fillius
> antique vendor

A one-stop shop featuring three floors and 40 dealers, the Antique Mall offers, well, just about anything.

"From sock monkeys to rhinestone jewelry and vintage clothing, it's like a bunch of miniature shops within a shop," says antique vendor and local artist Jenny Fillius. "It's so much fun to go looking around because you never know what you're going to find. It's like a hunt."

And while you stroll the stalls you can't help but walk down memory lane.

"One neat thing about the Antique Mall is that you'll see something you parted with as a child or something your parents used to own and realize that it actually has value today," says Mary Lou Williams, a shop volunteer at Emilie's Treasures.

But even though the merchandise is technically "old," the selection is surprisingly fresh and new.

"With so many dealers, we see new things every day," says owner Katherine Detore. "It's really fun because it's so eclectic."

But she advises shoppers to jump at the chance to buy if they see something they like because, unlike at department stores, the merchandise is often one of a kind or irreplaceable.

"Our philosophy is that, if you like it, you should buy an antique when you see it," she reflects. "Because oftentimes when people come back, it's gone."

While you could spend hours in the Antique Mall alone, if you'd like to try another venue, consider the Admiralty House. Owned and operated by Fred and Marge Dau for close to four decades, this North Admiral shop is a West Seattle icon.

Specializing in vintage Christmas items, picture frames, tools, and other collectibles, the Admiralty House is a treasure in itself.

"My husband used to teach industrial art for years," explains Marge Dau. "So he appreciates tools and has collected them from all over."

Shoppers delight in the quality and quantity the Daus offer in a relatively small space.

What:
Go Antiquing

Where:
The Antique Mall
4516 California Ave
206.935.9774

Admiralty House Antiques
2141 California Ave
206.935.4195

When:
Antique Mall hours are
Monday–Saturday 10 am–6 pm
Sunday 11 am–5 pm

Admiralty House hours are
Thursday–Saturday 11 am–4 pm
Sunday 1–4 pm

Price:
Free to look

"The vintage Christmas ornaments are pretty spectacular," says Fillius. "I have never seen such a large selection in my life."

But they're not just pretty pieces—they are also precious remnants of the past.

"The great thing about collectors is that they are holding onto pieces of our history for us," beams Fillius.

So whether you're hoping for a mini history lesson, aiming to buy "recycled" gifts, or just looking to spend a couple hours trying something new, check out West Seattle's older side and go antiquing.

66 | Get Crafty at Friends and Company

From the outside, passersby may simply see stacks of small wooden blocks. Aisles lined with wood-handled rubber stamps—a secret wall of images just waiting to be turned over and brought to life. Step inside, and you'll see that Friends and Company is a whole lot more than a stamp store.

Up in the art loft, a women's group is busily beading, while down on the main floor owner Doris Goulet is preparing for the evening's back-to-back scrapbooking, card-making, and batik print classes.

A fun, productive place to spend a day or evening while learning to make your own gifts, greeting cards, jewelry, stationery, books, and more, Friends and Company offers not only craft supplies but also a busy calendar of classes to get in touch with your own creativity.

You can get crafty four days a week (and sometimes more) with classes for students of all ages and interests. But where does one begin?

Goulet suggests taking a beginner class to get a feel for what she offers. Beginner card-making is a great way to start. Appropriately titled, "In the Beginning," this class teaches the steps to making professional-looking greeting cards using rubber stamps. Goulet begins by thanking her students for coming but promptly warns first-timers, "Watch out, because this can be addictive."

The class features four projects organized in a stair-step method to start off easy and work into more complex activities. The first card project introduces the student to the environment and the tools and then lets them simply color in the images made from the rubber stamp (aka "coloring 101").

> **"Watch out, because this can be addictive."**
>
> Doris Goulet
> owner

"We have never had a better excuse to go back to second grade and color

until taking up the art of rubber stamping," smiles Goulet.

The second project teaches the technique of "masking"—adding depth and dimension to the piece. The third project features embossing to add shine and texture. And the final project shows how simple folds and stamped art can turn a regular envelope into a decorative gift bag. At the end, students walk away with three cool cards, a gift bag, and the knowledge to come back and do it again on their own.

You can sign up as an individual or book entire groups. Many people create their own events and hold classes for birthday parties. It's also just a good excuse to get your friends together to do something fun while releasing your inner artist.

"There's something fun for everybody," says Goulet. "We have every generation here."

So it's not uncommon to see kids, young adults, moms, dads, and seniors. And whatever craft you choose, you are sure to create unique results.

"The best thing about what we do here is that it lets people's individual creativity exude," nods Goulet.

Keep company with friends at Friends and Company and you'll discover what can happen when you unleash your creative side.

What:
Friends and Company
Craft Classes

Where:
4540 California Ave SW
www.friends-n-company.com
206.932.3891

When:
Monday–Friday 10 am–7 pm
Saturday 10 am–5 pm
Sunday Noon–4 pm

See website for class schedules

Price:
See website for class prices

67 | Underground Tunes at Flying Lion

Good music, comfy couches, and sinful desserts—all in a church basement?

That's right. Welcome to Flying Lion Café, a coffeehouse music venue located below Doxa Church on 35th Avenue. The Flying Lion, owned by the church above, is a non-profit weekend music venue, café, and neighborhood hangout open to the public.

People of all ages and walks of life flock to the bohemian underground oasis for everything from jazz to electric pop to alt country. There is no cover charge as the musicians play for free. The menu simply says, "Please tip the musicians. They love to play but they like to eat too!"

> *"The people are here because they want to experience community and be connected with those they live near. This is something our society is longing for, and some are finding it here."*
>
> Adam Hendrix
> manager

In addition to music, Café Vita espresso drinks, hot fudge sundaes, and burgers, the Flying Lion also offers three free computer stations, WiFi Internet access, and rotating art exhibits.

Named for the mythical character Aslan from C.S. Lewis' *Chronicles of Narnia*, the Flying Lion was a coffeehouse vision that's taken off, even in its underground location.

Before the lion roared, the church was renting out unneeded space here and there to different organizations. But with the help of church members and Pastor Bill Clem, an idea became reality—a unique place for community to gather and a safe, not to mention fun, place for people of all ages to go.

"The décor is welcoming, the food delicious, and the music entertain-

ARTS & ENTERTAINMENT

ing, but the one thing that separates this café from any other place is the people," explains manager Adam Hendrix. "The people are here because they want to experience community and be connected with those they live near. This is something our society is longing for, and some are finding it here."

It's a place where people come and meet their neighbors again, a place to feel like part of a community—one neighbor at a time. From new moms to seniors, the audience is all across the board. And the teens and tweens are also discovering there's finally a place to hang out after most places close.

Whoever happens to follow their curiosity and wander in seems to find ownership in discovering this unique "underground" oasis.

So instead of "flying" by the Lion next time you're on 35th, venture down the stairs into this musical coffeehouse for good eats, fine tunes, and a bit of community refuge.

What:
Flying Lion Café

Where:
7551 35th Ave SW
(below the Doxa Church)
www.flyinglioncafé.com
206.932.0435

When:
Friday & Saturday 6 pm–midnight
Sunday 6:30–8:30 pm

Price:
No cover; menu items vary

68 | Cooking Parties with Culinary Communion

Ever wanted to throw a fiesta featuring Spanish tapas and paella? How about a hand-rolled sushi soiree complete with sake?

Many love the social aspect of having people over to eat, but the preparation, cooking, and timing of it all can be overwhelming. And if you've never made a particular dish before, testing it out at a dinner party can be stressful and challenging.

That's where West Seattle's own Culinary Communion comes in. Bringing parties together in the comfort of your home or theirs, Culinary Communion (CC) chefs provide the food and any out-of-the-ordinary appliances while teaching you and your friends how to make whatever your dinner party crowd desires.

These cooking parties, or in-home cooking classes, let you learn how to prepare wonderful new foods in a casual atmosphere where wine and beer flow as freely as the friendly conversation.

"In such a comfortable environment, participants really don't have the 'I'm in school' sense," says Culinary Communion co-owner Heidi Kenyon. "They can drink wine, laugh, and they actually pick up on things better because the class is really shaped to what they want to get out of it."

> *"Sushi parties are fun because we're just rolling and chatting, chatting and rolling."*
>
> Heidi Kenyon
> co-owner

Kenyon and her husband chef Gabriel Claycamp (a graduate of the Culinary Institute of America in Hyde Park) started Culinary Communion after an interesting conversation at the Seattle Cooks Show. The couple had an idea, but no location at the time, and an anxious student asked, "Could you come teach classes at my house?"

"We went with it and things have been going like hotcakes ever since," smiles Kenyon.

In-house cooking parties are a great way to spend a birthday, anniversary, holiday business party, or bridal shower. Some of the more popular items to include on the menus are Thai food and sushi rolls.

"Sushi parties are fun because we're just rolling and chatting, chatting and rolling," says Kenyon.

But clients can be as creative as their taste buds fancy. Some opt for Valentine's chocolate-making, holiday spirits-blending, or private wine and cheese education classes.

"One of our more interesting themes of late was an 'Olfactory Assault' party," describes Kenyon. "We had to cook all sorts of stinky, smelly—but good—foods such as Vietnamese spring rolls in a fish dipping sauce, salad with Muenster cheese crostini croutons, and lamb with roasted garlic."

And in the case of this theme, if you'd rather get out of the house, Culinary Communion will invite you to theirs.

"We have a great house with a newly remodeled kitchen and a view," says Kenyon. "In fact, we host a lot of our classes here."

Whether you want to mingle in your place or theirs, Culinary Communion will bring your party together for good company and fine foods that you all learn to prepare together.

What a fine set-up to say, "Bon appetit!"

What:
Cooking Parties

Where:
Your house, or Culinary Communion House
www.culinarycommunion.com
206.284.8687

When:
See website

Price:
Varies

69 | Discover West Seattle's Thrift Shops

Looking for a good old secondhand sweater? Or a one-of-a-kind gift with a hint of history? The Westside is the place if you want to get thrifty. According to thrift store connoisseurs, West Seattle is an untapped market for unique and inexpensive items.

> *"West Seattle's a gold mine."*
>
> Amy Ludwig
> Many Moons Trading Co.

"Not only do the trendy thrift shops in Fremont and Capitol Hill mark up their items, but the really good stuff is picked over," says Amy Ludwig of Many Moons Trading Co. "West Seattle's a gold mine."

West Seattle thrift shops also offer a lot in terms of quality.

"Because West Seattle is one of the largest residential neighborhoods in Seattle, we end up with a lot of quality goods," concurs Backstage Thrift owner Greg Kerton, who also owns a thrift shop on Capitol Hill.

And you can feel good about buying because each shop benefits a charity. Here's a rundown of the main selection.

Backstage Thrift
One of the only thrift stores to benefit the arts, Backstage Thrift's proceeds go to the Northwest Actors Studio. Backstage offers mostly clothes, some housewares, and a $5 vintage rack that "is just awesome," vows Kerton.

Discovery Shop
Benefiting the American Cancer Society, the Discovery Shop is operated completely by volunteers. Offering mostly clothing and jewelry, the business is otherwise known as an "upscale resale shop."

"We have so many regulars that it feels like a country store where people buy or just stop into visit," says shop volunteer Eloise Peters.

Many Moons Trading Co.
In the heart of the Junction, at the end of a narrow, winding hallway, you'll discover a secondhand gem in Many Moons.

"This place is kind of like magic," smiles manager Emily Williamson. "Little miracles happen here all the time."

Offering clothing, jewelry, Native American art, a $1 room, and a popular "free" box, this thrift shop benefits elders at the Pine Ridge Reservation in South Dakota.

Stop & Shop

A thrift shop run to support West Seattle's Senior Center, Stop & Shop offers an array of items from clothing to games to furniture.

"If it's in good shape, we'll take it," says volunteer Bob Kirvy.

Emilie's Treasures

Located in Providence Mt. St. Vincent (a long-term care facility), Emilie's Treasures is named after Providence nun Emilie Gamlin. A social destination for residents, their families, and employees, this upscale thrift shop offers more than merchandise.

"A great many of our residents come by for daily hugs," says volunteer Mary Lou Williams.

It also serves as an inexpensive option for employees, many of whom have families outside the U.S.

"We have nearly 26 different nationalities working here," explains Williams. "And it's exciting to sell a nice scarf to someone, say, from Ethiopia, who will then send this gift home."

So whether you're out to find treasures or donate some of your own, West Seattle is the place to be when it comes to getting thrifty.

What:
Thrift Shopping

Where:
Backstage Thrift
4306 SW Oregon
206.937.1910

Discovery Shop
4535 California Ave
206.937.7169

Many Moons Trading Co.
4517 California Ave Suite B
206.937.3481

Stop & Shop
4217 SW Oregon
206.932.4044

Emilie's Treasures
4831 35th SW
206.937.3700

When:
Call as hours vary

Price:
Free to look

70 | Learn to Swing Dance

Every first and third Sunday of the month, something's swingin' inside an unassuming building in West Seattle. Open the door of the Alki Masonic Temple, and you'll discover a scene where music moves masses, men lead, and women always start with their right foot forward (good advice in any situation).

Welcome to West Coast Swing Dancing, put on by the Seattle Swing Dance Club.

"One, two, three, four, five, six," count the attentive students.

The club has been swinging for close to 40 years, and people come from all over to do it. Long-time club member Barbara Wettland, who hasn't missed a dance in 15 years, travels three hours each way to dance and mingle with life-long friends.

"I learned to do West Coast Swing in 1951. I'm still doing it, and I just turned 80," she smiles. "The original name of our club was the Single Swingers, but because of the name everybody thought it was a party, so we changed it to the Seattle Swing Dance Club."

Swing dance started on the East Coast in traditional ballrooms. When it became popular on the West Coast, the style evolved to accommodate smaller venues and "slot" dancing was developed. This means that, instead of dancing all over a wide, open floor, couples dance in their own area or "slot." This new style became known as West Coast Swing, which the Seattle Swing Dance Club is proud to teach you, no matter your age or experience level.

> *"It's exercise. It's social. And a good way to learn something new you can use for the rest of your life."*
>
> Bill Bevington
> club member

"We have members as young as 19 and some as old as 80-something," says member Bill Bevington. "I didn't dance a step until I was 39 and I am 53 now.

Once you start, your social life just explodes. You make all kinds of new friends, dance together, take trips together. It's great."

With his introduction to West Coast Swing, Bevington has found this dance to be a new way of life.

"It's exercise. It's social. And a good way to learn something new you can use for the rest of your life."

The evening starts with a beginning West Coast Swing lesson at 4 p.m., followed by the best swing dancing in Seattle from 5 p.m. to 9 p.m. And while official instruction ends at 5 p.m., there are plenty of experienced dancers who will gladly guide you through the night—teaching you how to count, improve your rendition of the "sugar push," and do the "left side pass" with attitude and grace.

So come on by and give it a try. Even if you don't think dancing's your thing, you may change your mind after learning to swing.

What:
Learn to Swing Dance

Where:
Alki Masonic Lodge
4736 40th Ave SW
www.seattlewcswing.org

When:
1st & 3rd Sunday
of the month
Lesson 4–5 pm
Dance 5–9 pm

Price:
$9 for visitors
$5 for club members

71 | Trick or Treat Fun for Kids

Kids of the Westside, count your blessings (and your candy pile), because West Seattle is a happenin' hood come Halloween. With events running all around the neighborhood, make sure to catch at least one for some serious Halloween hoopla.

Admiral Isle Halloween Treats and Treasures

Put on your pirate costumes and head to Admiral for the annual Admiral Isle Halloween Treats and Treasures event. When the time draws near, simply keep your eyes and ears open for details and pick up the Admiral Isle Treasure Map & Treat Bag at participating businesses (you'll bring this along to hunt for your bounty).

> *With candy already in hand and a chance to win big—how can you lose?*

The hunt starts at a designated destination (usually Metropolitan Market). Then you just follow the map, picking up treats, and stamping your map at each store. Once you've collected as many stamps as you can, you enter to win a treasure chest of treats.

With candy already in hand and a chance to win big on top of that—how can you lose?

Trick or Treat in the Alaska Junction

For years, Trick or Treat in the Junction has been the gathering place for daytime candy-collecting fun from local merchants. Gaggles of costumed girls and boys take over the streets. The sidewalks swell with an unintentional parade of miniature Batmen, Care Bears, scarecrows, and more. Each merchant offers a special treat, including ice cream from Husky Deli.

"We average between 1,500 and 3,000 kids each year," says Kay Knapton, former executive director of the Junction Association. "It's so popular now, we start getting calls in September."

West Seattle kids are lucky to have so much ghoul and goblin fun right in their own backyard, as many kids travel miles for the event.

"We have kids coming all the way from Marysville and Puyallup," explains Knapton. "Families schedule full day visits to friends' houses here around this event."

Parents like it because it's a safe way to introduce kids to Halloween. Kids like it because, well, there's candy! Oh, and costumes. And fun.

The Farmers Market's Annual Pumpkin Decorating

Every year on the Sunday closest to Halloween, from 10 a.m.-2 p.m., the Farmers Market hosts a pumpkin-decorating contest for kids.

When the treat bags begin to bust from candy cargo overload, the makeup begins to itch, and the costumes have had their flaunting, this event offers a more organic way to experience the holiday. For the duration of Farmers Market hours, kids can explore their creative side and decorate pumpkins to celebrate. Bring your cameras, 'cause this one is fun—and a good way to get pumpkin decorating ideas for next year!

What:
Trick or Treating

Where:
Admiral Junction Treasure Hunt
Metropolitan Market
206.937.0551

Alaska Junction Trick or Treat
www.wsjunction.com
206.935.0904

Farmer's Market Pumpkin Decorating
www.seattlefarmersmarkets.org

When:
Event dates vary; see websites and numbers above for details

Price:
Free

72 | Seattle Music Fest at Alki

Summer sun shines. Guitars strum. And an enthralled audience sways with feet in the sand. It's tough to beat good music on a beautiful beach with an amazing sunset encore each night.

For more than a decade West Seattle's been home to the Seattle Music Fest at Alki Beach, put on by Northwest Programs for the Arts (NPA) and generous sponsorship from the community.

And while this festival is relatively new in a typical West Seattleite's view, the tradition of summer tunes on Alki hearkens back nearly a century.

"Alki Beach has a musical history that began in the early 1900s," explains NPA Executive Director Adam Sheridan. "There were summer concerts every Sunday on a bandstand that stood out over water near the present-day Statue of Liberty."

Over the years, concerts came and went and were revived a few times in '60s and '70s. But Lady Liberty beckoned the music back for the current iteration of the festival today.

The Seattle Music Fest at Alki Beach actually began after the Statue of Liberty was vandalized—the event was organized to raise money to recast her. The festival was so well received that it's been returning to the beach ever since, introducing current music styles through this long-standing Alki tradition.

> ## "Alki Beach has a musical history that began in the early 1900s."
>
> Adam Sheridan
> NPA Executive Director

"The festival showcases emerging bands for growing fans as well as a non-clubbing audience that would otherwise not have a chance to see them," explains Sheridan. "It's a low-cost, one-stop way to sample the menu of new music in the Northwest in a weekend."

Past performers have included, Aqueduct (now playing at the Sasquatch Music Fest), Ian Moore, Dolour, the Latin pop/rock fusion of

Quasi Nada, South Africa's top artist Karma, the female-fronted pop band Honey Tongue, Mike Doughty from Soul Coughing, Carrie Akre, and Cee-lo Green. Names are getting bigger each year, and so is the event.

"The festival has grown from a little stage with barely a sound system to a professional festival that people come from out of town just to attend," beams Sheridan. "And you can't blame them. There is no more beautiful spot in the city to have an outdoor concert. Hearing great music with this beautiful backdrop just makes people's eyes light up."

Almost like magic, Alki offers its typical atmosphere one day, and the next day, the beach is filled with melodies and wide-smiling music-lovers.

And although the festival features current music styles, the event attracts all ages.

"You'll see everything from teens with tattoos and piercings to old couples tapping their toes in the sand," says Sheridan. "There's nothing like it."

What:
Seattle Music Fest at Alki

Where:
Alki Beach (right next to the Alki Bathhouse Art Studio)
www.seattlemusicfest.org
866.208.6293

When:
Usually the second weekend of August; check website for dates
www.northwestarts.org

Price:
Suggested donation of $5; more is always appreciated

73 | Outdoor Sidewalk Cinema

Looking for a fun Friday night activity to do outside with the family? Come see the stars under the stars each summer at West Seattle's outdoor sidewalk cinema "Movies on the Wall."

> *See the stars under the stars each summer.*

The action takes place in the historic brick courtyard on the corner of California and Genesee. Sidewalk Cinema projects films onto the north side of the post office wall while the audience sits in the parking lot of the original site for the Seattle Lighting Company. Built in 1910, the location has been part of West Seattle history for nearly a century.

Drawn to this true community event, moviegoers begin to gather around 7:45 p.m. to set up prime viewing spots. And part of the fun is learning new ways to be creative with your cinema comforts. You see everything from sleeping bags and lawn chairs to gourmet picnic dinners. So bring whatever makes you comfy for the show (no glass, please).

Once you are situated, just sit back and enjoy the pre-show entertainment, such as live music, raffles, magic tricks, silent shorts, and cartoons. The films begin just after dusk.

Featured movies are always family-friendly—past flicks have included titles like *Babe, Willy Wonka and the Chocolate Factory, Star Wars,* and *The Wizard of Oz.*

The movie choices are a reflection of the organizer's personal tastes as well as a compilation of what other outdoor cinemas choose throughout the county.

"The community loves to be involved," explains Amy Derenthal, capital campaign manager for the Senior Center of West Seattle.

So how did Sidewalk Cinema come to be?

It all began when Dr. Jim Pierce moved his practice into the old mortuary building on the classic Westside corner. His wife Julie took one look at the post office wall on the south end of the parking lot and decided they had to do something with this great space. Native West Seattleites, the couple felt it was important to be a part of the community and wanted to hold events that represent their commitment to this idea.

The brainchild of Julie Pierce, West Seattle's Sidewalk Cinema began shortly thereafter, sponsored by the practice of Doctors Jim Pierce and Heidi Horwitz as well as many area businesses. Movies are offered for free to the public while the sales of concessions and "pass the hat" donations go to local charities like West Seattle Senior Center, Westside Baby, and the West Seattle Helpline. It's a win-win-win situation for everyone involved.

Buoyed by an enthusiasm akin to nostalgia for drive-in movies of the '50s and '60s, outdoor cinema is a growing trend in communities throughout the country. And with audiences of up to 175 people at the north junction, West Seattle's Sidewalk Cinema is no exception.

So stroll on down, snuggle up, and get ready for films that are as classic as the brick courtyard itself—and don't forget to BYOC (bring your own chair)!

What:
Outdoor Sidewalk Cinema

Where:
4400 California Ave SW
www.sidewalkcinema.com
or www.wsjunction.com

When:
Fridays & Saturdays 9 pm
June–Aug (rescheduled if drizzly); check websites for schedule

Price:
Free (donations suggested)

74 | Take Back Your Time

When is the last time someone asked "how are you?" and you did not reply "busy"?

Do you find yourself paging through your calendar weeks in advance just to schedule coffee with a friend? How often do you need a weekend to recover from your weekend of running around doing errands to catch up from the workweek?

Sound familiar? You are not alone.

What experts refer to as "time poverty" looms in the streets of West Seattle and nationwide. Mandatory overtime is at historically high levels. Each year the average American works 350 hours more than the average Western European. And such frenzy continues to increase. Work weeks run longer and vacations get cut shorter, if they're taken at all.

But for at least one day each year, there's something you can do to keep from becoming a victim of time burglary.

Introducing Take Back Your Time Day.

A non-partisan national initiative with some of its strongest supporters rooted right here in West Seattle, Take Back Your Time Day calls attention to the problems of overwork, over-scheduling, and time poverty that now threaten America's health, family life, civic life, and environment.

For one day each year, starting today in fact, there's something you can do to keep from becoming a victim of time burglary.

The date of the annual event falls on October 24th, exactly nine weeks before the end of the year, signifying the additional amount of time each year that Americans work above and beyond their European counterparts.

"We're hoping to spark a national conversation about overwork and time pressure in America," says Take Back Your Time Day National Coordinator John de Graaf (de Graaf also edited the initiative's official handbook). "Something like what the discussion of Earth Day did for the environment," he explains.

De Graaf is an independent documentary filmmaker at KCTS TV and an author known best for his book *Affluenza: The All-Consuming Epidemic* and the film that went with it. Many of de Graaf's cohorts in the movement hail from West Seattle: Dr. Steven Bezruchka of UW School of Public Health; Paul Loeb, author of *Soul of a Citizen: Living with Conviction in a Cynical Time*; and Doug Frick, a video producer. And these local activists are making their mark on the nation, even in the eyes of skeptics.

While many may argue that working less is bad for business, Time Day supporters such as Sharon Lobel of Seattle University's Albers School of Business believe that working less is actually good for business. According to Lobel, working fewer hours fosters more loyal workers. Employees feel better about the work they're doing and better in general, causing fewer health expenses, less absenteeism, and more creativity in the workplace.

What can a West Seattleite do? How about the 100 other activities that appear in these pages? Whether you choose to do one a week or one a month, spending your precious time on activities outside of work and in your community is a conscious, healthy choice. Of course, you don't have to wait until October, either. You can take your finger off the fast-foward button whenever you like—starting right now.

What:
Take Back Your Time Day

Where:
West Seattle, or wherever you live
www.timeday.org

When:
Each year on October 24

Price:
Free

75 | Get to Know Your Neighbor at the Junction Festival

Chocolate-dipped bananas. Packs of face-painted kids. And street-dancing denizens.

Sound like fun? It is. But this festive atmosphere only happens once a year—when the West Seattle Junction Festival is on.

> *"Think of the festival as an excuse to get to know your community."*
>
> Sherry Fadely
> Festival Coordinator

Hosted by the Junction Association and held in conjunction with the Junction Merchants' Sidewalk Sale, this neighborhood gathering amasses the masses for three full days of family-friendly fun. It takes place every July and has grown to become one of the area's biggest and best summer street fair traditions.

"It's a family-oriented event with community ties that are stronger than ever," smiles festival coordinator Sherry Fadely.

The festival began as a merchants' sidewalk sale in 1963 and was founded by long-time merchant Margaret Miaullis, who basically ran the show until she retired at age 85. The sale became an annual event and in 1980 expanded to include arts and crafts. Before long, Miaullis applied for permits and began closing off the street to traffic, making the event an official street festival in 1983.

Kids' events such as the Big Wheel Race added fun to the festival, and each year came something new, from splash dunk tanks and pony rides to petting zoos and inflatable castles.

Adults' events such as baking contests also added flavor to the fest. And along with flavor, came culture. Live music and entertainment began, and a beer garden sprouted up. This last combination brought about the famed street dance.

The biggest event of its kind in West Seattle, today the festival attracts more than 30,000 people. It features over 150 art and craft vendors, 20 food booths, two stages with continuous live entertainment, a beer and wine garden, a children's play area, a Sunday Farmers Market, and, of course, the traditional Saturday Night Street Dance.

And as the neighborhood evolves, the festival grows with the community.

"It's getting more eclectic each year," describes Fadely. "The food and music are more diverse, and it's expanding in all ways imaginable—from booth content to the actual festival area."

The event recently grew to the north, adding a second stage and more merchants.

"But it's not just about quantity," says Fadely. "It's also about quality. We are focusing on special attractions each day with a great lineup of professional musicians from jazz and bluegrass to sought-after comedic performers like the Zambini Brothers and the Valentine Performing Pigs."

And though names and faces change from year to year, the festival's ongoing goal is to grow and improve by getting the community more involved.

What:
West Seattle Junction Festival

Where:
West Seattle Junction (from Edmunds to Oregon on California Ave, and from 42nd to 44th on Alaska St.)
www.wsjunctionfestival.com
206.353.7635

When:
Mid–July; check yearly for specific dates

Price:
Free

"This festival brings in people from well beyond West Seattle," explains Fadely. "But its success starts from the inside with community-driven support and positive energy. If anything, think of the festival as an excuse to get to know your community."

So consider attending the festival as a way to connect with your neighbors each year. Or even go and volunteer. You might be surprised how the junction comes alive when you're a part of the action in the heart of West Seattle.

76 | Stroll the Alki Open Market

When it comes to summertime, West Seattleites live for the weekend. And while many may get their duties of domesticity done during the week in order free up Saturday and Sunday for fun and sun, there's now a reason to save your shopping for the weekend and combine it with a day at the beach.

Introducing the Alki Beach Open Market.

Just steps away from the mile-plus stretch of sand, south of Coastal Surf Boutique, the Alki Beach Open Market is a fun way to spend a weekend day shopping outdoors without crossing the bridge to Pike Place.

9 a.m. until 3 p.m. every Saturday and Sunday from late spring till fall, you can stroll the stalls filled with colorful arts and crafts.

> **"We have so many people coming through Alki, walking the beach with coffee in hand, and now, on top of scenery itself, there is something for people to look at and do."**
>
> Bryan Pennington
> market manager

The market is a mecca for a myriad of interesting artists and feels like an open-air invite into their creative studios. You'll find everything from embroidered jean jackets to Peruvian pan flutes to handmade soaps and fresh-cut flowers. The broad selection complements the beach's other offerings and adds a unique, local flavor to the scene.

"It's a great mix of vendors in a prime location," says market manager Bryan Pennington. "And the casual, open air atmosphere is only fitting when you're down on the beach. People just wander in and out, from stall to stall, chatting with vendors while soaking up the sun. It's really fun."

A welcome addition to laying out or eating out, it also gives the beach's swarms of visitors something to do, something to see—something uniquely Alki Beach.

"We have so many people coming through Alki, walking the beach with coffee in hand, and now, on top of scenery itself, there is something for people to look at and do," says Pennington.

But shoppers aren't the only ones enjoying the market.

"There's a great feeling in the air because vendors and visitors alike just love being here," continues Pennington. "With the views of the Olympic Mountains and the Sound, there's no better 'office' or shopping environment around."

The Alki Beach Open Market also features a silent auction section where the public can participate by selling furniture, antiques, and other quality goods—a great option when you're not up for putting on a full-scale garage sale.

Pennington compares it to a live version of eBay, only better. "Here, it's convenient and you also get to see, touch, and feel the items before you buy them."

"It's the perfect opportunity to offload that beautiful end table that you just couldn't give away," he smiles.

What:
Alki Beach Open Market

Where:
2530 Alki Ave SW
206.935.0142

When:
Saturday
11am-5pm
Throughout Summer

Price:
Free to look

A bustling display of sights, sounds, and scents, the beach market adds yet another layer of vibrancy, soul, and depth to the cultural evolution of West Seattle. So whether you're in the market for stall-to-stall shopping or you're the silent auction type, the Alki Beach Open Market awaits.

Sifu Restita DeJesus of Yin Yang Arts Center leads her
Saturday morning tradition of "Tai Chi on the Beach."

ENRICHMENT

In West Seattle you will find a world of opportunities in education and
self-improvement—for mind, body, and soul. From learning to blow
molten glass to karate with the kids, here are 24 ways to enrich your life
on the Westside whether you're a life-long resident or tourist for the day.

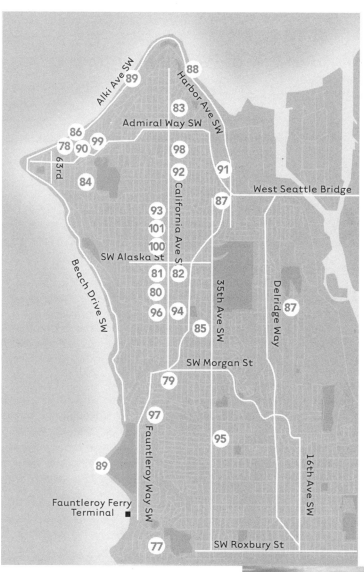

Alki Ave SW

89

88

Harbor Ave SW

83

Admiral Way SW

86

78 90 99

98

92

91

63rd

84

West Seattle Bridge

87

California Ave SW

93

101

100

SW Alaska St

81 82

80

96 94

35th Ave SW

85

Beach Drive SW

Deridge Way

87

SW Morgan St

79

97

95

89

Fauntleroy Way SW

16th Ave SW

Fauntleroy Ferry
Terminal ■

77

SW Roxbury St

77 | Beat Bad-Weather Blues with Group Cycling

When winter winds whip through West Seattle and the sky is as dark when you leave for work as it is when you get home, many bicyclists tend to develop a case of the bad-weather blues.

> *"Let's put on a little heavy metal and get angry."*
>
> Cory Bibby
> instructor

But do not fret. Even in the pouring rain, there is hope. It's called group cycling at the Fauntleroy YMCA.

An indoor biking class otherwise known as "spinning," group cycling keeps you in shape during the off-season without freezing your toes and nose off. And the open windows bring in cool breezes and the fresh scent of surrounding evergreens, providing an outdoor sensation while you spin away in the comfort of a warm, friendly room.

For those who have never spun before, here's how it works. Each bike is stationary and includes a special knob attached to the frame that is cranked clockwise to increase resistance and counterclockwise for easier pedaling. The instructor takes you on a "ride" that may include hills (high resistance), sprints (low resistance and high cadence), flats (medium cadence and resistance), and isolation exercises to target specific muscles. All of this is done in a casual, comfortable atmosphere to an eclectic mix of inspiring tunes.

"Let's put on a little heavy metal and get angry," smiles instructor Cory Bibby as he pumps up the group for a big hill section.

Bibby varies his music selection to fit the intensity of the workout, and people of all ages get into the groove while they catch up on the week's events between breaths.

"We like to joke around, but we're still working out and getting in shape," says Bibby. "Everybody supports each other and has a good time."

Bibby's been on the bike for years, starting with BMX racing as a child, then mountain-cross and downhill with his team, Speed Metal Racing. But don't worry—you aren't expected to keep up with Cory. In fact, you don't even have to be a cyclist to enjoy the class.

"It's great exercise that anyone can do," encourages Bibby. "My students are about fifty-fifty when it comes to cyclists and non-cyclists. We have a bike messenger and a guy who has ridden the course of the Tour de France, as well as people who have never been on a road bike before."

Others are test-driving the class as their introduction to the sport.

"Taking this class is motivating me to learn how to ride outside," says spinner Colleen Nickel.

And if she keeps spinning at this rate, by spring she'll be passing those cyclists who took the winter off. Not a Y member? No worries; this class is open to the public for a day fee or you can simply buy a punch card. Next time the winter weather blues come knocking, just give them the slip with a ride inside.

What:
Group Cycling

Where:
Fauntleroy YMCA
9260 California Ave
www.seattleymca.org
206.937.1000

When:
Monday & Wednesday 5:45–6:45pm
Tuesday & Thursday 5:45 am–6:45 am
Saturday 9:15 am–10:15 am

Price:
$8 per class or
$50 punch card good for 8 visits

78 | Peer into the Past at Log House Museum

Step inside the Log House Museum and step back into West Seattle history. Feel the hardwood floors creak beneath your feet and sense the solid log walls that surround you as you peer into the past. From the giant wooden wheel of the 1909 steamship *Kennedy* to the bathing suits worn by brave pioneers who swam for pleasure in the chilly waters off Alki, this time capsule of local treasures is not only the historical icon of the neighborhood but also the birthplace of Seattle.

"If you look up the history of Seattle, this is what you'll find," smiles long-time volunteer Carol Vincent.

> ## "If you look up the history of Seattle, this is what you'll find."
>
> Carol Vincent
> volunteer

Just steps away from Alki, where in1851 the schooner *Exact's* landing party planted the seed for this city, the building of the current Log House Museum commenced when settlers moved into the area.

The past 150-odd years of West Seattle's history are captured within the walls of the museum, and the building itself is one of the most prized pieces of the "collection."

Built by the Bernard family over a century ago as part of the Fir Lodge Estate, the Log House Museum was originally used as an outbuilding for horses and carriages. After the estate sold, the building was a family home and antique store until the Southwest Seattle Historical Society purchased it in 1994 to create the museum.

"People are surprised when they walk in the door. It's sort of unexpected that this house is such a piece of Seattle history," explains Vincent. "They love to touch the logs."

Heralded by King County as "the most successful heritage acquisition project in King County history," the museum offers many ways to educate and entertain visitors.

Historical Flicks

Film fans can cozy up on the corner bench and learn about Native Americans and the landing party by watching *Alki: The Birthplace of Seattle* along with other locally produced pieces on area history.

Tours by Local Experts

Get a veteran tour guide going, and you won't believe all the interesting things that once happened here. The museum offers historical interpretation tours for school groups and other organizations.

Local Learning Tools

The Log House Museum also offers heritage education kits including reproduced maps, photos, documents, and artifacts along with lesson plans and activities. Additional books and videos are also available for rental.

Gift Shop

Out back, next to the garden of native plants, the museum also runs a gift shop. Many books written by local authors are available in addition to vintage postcards, mugs, and other Seattle-themed gifts.

What:
Log House Museum

Where:
3003 61st Ave SW
www.loghousemuseum.org
206.938.5293

When:
Thursday Noon–6 pm
Saturday & Sunday Noon–3 pm

Price:
Admission by donation
(suggested donation:
$3 adult, $1 children)

For visitors and West Seattleites alike, this is a one-of-a-kind way to play tourist for a day.

"The Log House offers a piece of history that would not exist without the museum," says Vincent. "Here, everybody can discover their roots."

So if you're curious about what Alki was like before rollerblades and bass stereos, pay a visit to the Log House. If only those logs walls could talk…

79 | Make Food Fun with NuCulinary

You gather around the table with fork in hand. A fabulous meal awaits you, and a friendly gentleman asks, "Can I pour you some merlot?" Nope, it's not a restaurant. Nor is it a wine tasting.

> *"My mission is to have fun with food!"*
>
> Naomi Kakiuchi
> owner & chef

It's Morgan Street Thriftway, and the feast is a sumptuous meal you made yourself with help from celebrated chef Naomi Kakiuchi, RD, CD. For years, Kakiuchi's been busy cooking up something special that's popular with West Seattle foodies and kitchen novices alike.

The name of the mouthwatering game: NuCulinary.

NuCulinary offers cooking classes in an intimate, interactive setting. Thanks to a limited class size, students work closely with Kakiuchi and other guest chefs to create wholesome, healthy meals that just happen to be delicious.

From pie making and knife skills to the art of sushi, NuCulinary features both demo and hands-on classes for kids and adults, as well as lessons in food history, preparation techniques, nutrition, safety, buying on a budget, and feeding the family.

"My mission is to have fun with food!" explains Kakiuchi.

And you can't help but have a few laughs along the way. Her wine-toting sidekick Wayton Lim certainly helps Kakiuchi entertain. When Lim was asked his official title at NuCulinary he smiled. "You can call me what you want," he said "but just don't call me late for dinner, at least not in this household."

Kakiuchi assures, "Oh, he's never late for dinner, believe me." And neither would you be if you sampled her fine fare.

With over 20 years of experience in the industry, Kakiuchi offers expertise that provides students with everything from nutrition facts to food product history (just ask her about the tortillas and lard story).

ENRICHMENT

She also favors a practical approach to enjoyable results, always taking students' busy schedules into consideration. "Our goal is to make your life simpler," she say.

"I like to give recipes for things you can often just pull out of your refrigerator or your pantry," she explains. "You know, things you have on hand right now that you can put together in a moment."

But cooking with NuCulinary isn't limited to the home. You can also bring food fun into the workplace. The company offers corporate events and teambuilding, including off-site cooking parties, project kickoffs, and special business bonding experiences to improve group trust and communication through cooking.

"Cooking is an innovative yet familiar way to learn problem-solving and leadership skills while inspiring creativity—all in a group environment," Kakiuchi says. "Often we integrate spouses and friends for a fun social aspect, too."

And NuCulinary doesn't stop at the workweek. You'll find Kakiuchi spreading the joy of cooking on the weekend at the Farmers Market, too. All summer long on Sundays in the Junction from 10 a.m. to 2 p.m., you will find her (or one of her staff) conducting cooking demos on fresh and seasonal produce, and handing out recipes to market shoppers.

"I want to put the fun back into food," smiles Kakiuchi. "In every aspect of people's lives—at home, in the office, and when they go out to play."

What:
Cooking Classes (for individuals or businesses)

Where:
NuCulinary (West Seattle Thriftway and elsewhere)
www.nuculinary.com
206.932.3855

When:
Call or check the website for details

Price:
Check the website as classes vary

80 | Bring Art to Life at Northwest Art & Frame

West Seattle is a haven for art appreciation. Just stroll the streets on a dark night and witness the well-lit paintings and pictures that decorate the varied walls and halls of the Westside.

Art surrounds us. And though most of us don't own an original Picasso, there are plenty of things we do have worth displaying—if not for public critique at least for personal satisfaction. Gather some of those prized possessions and consider preserving them as a special piece you design yourself by learning to frame at Northwest Art & Frame in the Junction.

Northwest Art & Frame began nearly four decades ago as Hi Yu Art Center where art supplies were sold and crafts classes were taught. The shop eventually began custom framing and selling ready-made frames. Today the focus is still on art and framing, but the shop also offers a great selection of gifts, so you can frame your piece, wrap it, and find the perfect gift card all in one stop.

> **"You bring the art, and we bring the art to life."**
>
> Gloria DaPra
> designer

But according to founder Dan Reiner, the products are just a portion of what the store has to offer. "One of the greatest assets of this store is the employees. They offer years of experience, which is really helpful to the first-time framer," he nods.

Designer and framer extraordinaire Gloria DaPra couldn't agree more. "We're all artists here with backgrounds in everything from painting to photography," she explains. "This is what helps us help our customers create the best design for their personal needs."

The staff also encourages you to think outside the box. Framing isn't just about posters, prints, and paintings. Try floating a series of your children's color crayon drawings to brighten bedrooms. Mount a race number and medal from your first marathon. Preserve your well-deserved college diploma. Or, scour your photo collections for your favorite prints—you'll enjoy them a lot more when you don't have to pull out your dusty old album. Keepsakes that would otherwise remain sitting around in a drawer can be appreciated each day if you just take the time to frame them.

Once you have your art in hand, bring it in and the staff will help you select matting in complementary colors, stylish frames, and UV glass to protect your art. And before you know it, voila, you have a display-ready piece for your walls.

According to Reiner, this is the best part about learning to frame, "Once someone has come in and figured out how to do it, they are just so delighted with themselves. We even have a sticker to finish off your piece that says 'I framed it myself at Northwest Art & Frame.'"

"Even people who have never done this before can bring in a picture and walk out an hour later with something beautiful," adds DaPra. "You bring the art, and we bring the art to life."

What:
Learn to Frame

Where:
Northwest Art & Frame
4733 California Ave
www.nw-artandframe.com
206.937.5507

When:
Monday–Friday 9:30 am–9 pm
Saturday 9:30 am–6 pm
Sunday 11 am–5 pm

Price:
Materials cost, but learning is free

81 | *Tour the Historical Murals*

When you're poking around the Junction, take a peek at all sides of the buildings in West Seattle and you just might learn something.

West Seattle's historical murals are some of the best in the Northwest—earning the National Neighborhood of the Year Project in 1992. Commissioned in 1989, the murals depict the neighborhood's intriguing past.

> *Take a peek at all sides of the buildings in West Seattle and you just might learn something.*

For high-quality results, the community project called for experts continent-wide.

"We insisted on getting the best painters we could find nationwide," reflects mural coordinator Earl Cruzan. "We brought in muralists from as far as Louisiana and Newfoundland."

And before the painters arrived, over a year of scouting and research had to be done.

So get out in the fresh air and take a mural tour.

West Seattle Ferries
Located on California and Alaska, this mural depicts the first two ferries on Puget Sound. The boats made 8-minute runs between downtown Seattle and West Seattle's Duwamish Head from 1888 to 1921.

Midnight Call
Painted by local artist Don Barrie, this mural was created from an old photograph of a horse-drawn rig leaving the Junction Station from its mural location on 44th and Alaska.

Mosquito Boat Landing
Located on California and Alaska, this mural depicts a 1910 Sunday landing of the *S.S. Clan McDonald* at Alki. The paddle-wheel vessel provided the major form of "turn-of-the-century" transportation around Puget Sound.

The First Duwamish Bridge

Painted from a vantage at Pigeon Point, this mural on 44th and SW Edmunds depicts the sweeping view of the first bridge to West Seattle, which was built around 1910. The vast tide lines shown here were drained and filled to create Harbor Island.

Morgan Street Market

Located on Morgan Street and Fauntleroy Way, this mural depicts the shopping center, which opened in 1924 and was served by the Gatewood and Fauntleroy streetcars.

Alki in the Twenties

The name says it all. Located on Fauntleroy and Edmunds, this mural depicts a vintage Chevy, a panoramic view of Alki, and the home of pioneer realtor W.T. Campbell.

Tuesday's Bank Day

Anyone who can recollect school days of the '20s knows all about "bank day." This mural is located on California and Oregon and depicts a 1923 classroom as students line up to make "deposits."

The Hi-Yu Parade

Depicting one of Western Washington's oldest community celebrations, this mural is located on the post office wall between Oregon and Genesee on California. It features a 1973 Hi-Yu float.

The Old Mud Hole

Located on 44th and Alaska, this mural depicts the swimming pool in Lincoln Park, which was installed by local philanthropist Laurence Colman. Originally a tidegate filled the pool with saltwater from Puget Sound.

What:
Historical Murals

Where:
West Seattle (see street names above)
www.wschamber.com
206.932.5685

When:
Year-round

Price:
Free

Press Day

This mural depicts the web-fed Duplex press at *West Seattle Herald*, pre-WWII. It is located on 44th between Alaska and Edmunds.

You may have seen many of these history-rich paintings in passing. Take a thoughtful tour of all 10, and you'll feel just how present that history still is today.

82 | *Take It Off at Urban Striptease Aerobics*

Watch out West Seattle—wild things are afoot in the Junction. Gals are gathering by the dozens to rock the world, or shake up the neighborhood, at least.

They're peeling off pounds *and* clothes at Urban Fitness' most popular class: Urban Striptease Aerobics. Yep, the fitness craze in New York, L.A., Chicago, and Miami has hit Seattle. And Urban Fitness was the first health club in the Pacific Northwest to offer the class.

"We're definitely one of the hip and happening clubs," says club owner Tricia Murphy. "We try daring new things, and this is one of them." Good dancing, of course, takes time and training.

"All of my instructors have a dance background," explains Murphy, referring to "dance" dance, not stripping. "I am trained in classical ballet and the others have experience in modern dance, break dancing, and hip hop."

Urban striptease aerobics combines moves from strip tease with aerobic exercise for a uniquely energizing, not to mention sexy, full-body workout. And some say it's even improving areas of life outside the gym as well.

> *"You girls are all stripper hot! Woohoo! Let's dance."*
>
> Laura Dunham
> instructor

So, what actually goes on in a room full of aspiring strippers? First of all, no guys allowed (nor can passersby take a peek). The studio is located in the back of the club, safely screened from gawking onlookers. Inside, a comfortable atmosphere puts the ladies at ease. The lights are low, and a disco ball sets the scene.

Gals start out stretching then the music begins, and the instructor kicks off the class with some female bonding and positive reinforcement.

"You girls are all stripper hot!" shouts the instructor. "Woohoo! Let's dance."

Step by step, a full routine is taught in an hour's time. And believe it or not, it's a real workout. Participants lose weight and gain a better sense of self. From college students to housewives to schoolteachers, women of all walks take part.

And the class has received an amazing turnout and even has a waitlist due to demand.

"It's absolutely packed every class," nods Murphy. "We're seeing big groups of women coming all the way from Olympia, Tacoma, Federal Way, and more. This has become quite the evening activity."

After the class, many ladies head next door to the Rocksport for post-workout beverages. And often the students seem to get special treatment.

"Especially if they know where these ladies have just been, bar patrons often welcome the girls into what you could call a very friendly environment," smiles Murphy. "For some reason, there's an especially large contingency of men there, conveniently right after our class."

Those guys could be on to something.

If you're looking for a new workout that's definitely different from your average exercise class, consider Urban Striptease Aerobics. And take it off, West Seattle! The weight, that is.

What:
Urban Striptease Aerobics

Where:
Urban Fitness
4700 California Ave SW
www.urbanfitnessseattle.com
206.938.4119

When:
Wednesdays 7:30–8:30 pm

Price:
Classes are $15 per night

Restrictions:
Must be at least 18 years of age; pre-registration is required

83 | Treat Yourself at Head-to-Toe Day Spa

When it's time to relieve stress and escape a fast-paced city lifestyle, the last thing you want to do is drive into the congestion of Seattle, wait in traffic, and spend valuable time searching for paid parking in order to unwind at a luxurious city spa.

There's no need to go downtown when you can slow down and relax right here at West Seattle's own Head-to-Toe Day Spa—where your special treatments begin from the ground on up.

> **"It's very personal, like a home away from home with a truly peaceful ambience."**
>
> Patrice Wolanin
> manager

Just walk in the door and your senses awaken as you take in the aroma of essential oils wafting through a cozy space graced with trickling fountains.

"We're small, but we're intimate," says manager Patrice Wolanin. "It's very personal, like a home away from home with a truly peaceful ambience."

When it comes to treatments, the approach is definitely personal with multiple offerings from, yes, head to toe, including scalp massages and aromatic foot soaks. For everything in between, try a Tension Relief "Moor" Mud Wrap or one of many massages—relaxation, pregnancy, deep tissue, or heated stone. Or go for the "best facial in Seattle," according to a prestigious ranking by *Allure* magazine.

In addition, Head-to-Toe offers waxing, tinting, manicures, and pedicures as well as non-invasive skincare treatments that give visible results (such as micro-current facial lifting and Photo-Actif™ microderm abrasion).

The day spa also specializes in permanent cosmetic makeup derived from natural pigments. Procedures include permanent eyebrows, eye liner, lip liner, and color adjustment.

ENRICHMENT

And day spa indulgences are not just for the ladies. Head-to-Toe also offers a wide variety of treatments for men and a specific line of men's products such as the spa "starter kit."

For first-timers or those who have a tough time making decisions, a great option is a sampling of treatments like the decadent "Spa Indulgence," the house "Favorite," or the "Spa Classic."

So, if you're ready to relax and be pampered, don't go far. Just head for Head-to-Toe and leave your stress behind.

What:
Day Spa

Where:
Head-to-Toe Day Spa
2328 California Ave SW
www.Head2ToeDaySpa.com
206.938.9300

When:
Monday–Thursday10 am–8 pm
Friday 9 am–7 pm
Saturday 9 am–5 pm
Sunday Noon–6 pm

Price:
Please see "services menu" on
the website as prices vary

84 | *Yoga in the Garden*

You are surrounded by rhododendrons, Japanese maples, tulips, butterfly bushes (which really do attract butterflies), and huge clematis with fragrant white blossoms. Nope, it's not an arboretum. Nor is it your typical yoga studio. It's Yoga For Our Times—a virtual oasis uniquely designed to relax the body and the mind.

Simply arriving at this serene West Seattle sanctuary immediately calms the senses. Yoga For Our Times is located in the Hillcrest neighborhood (just over the crest from Genesee) and overlooks lush gardens and views of the Sound and the Olympic mountains.

"It's a little piece of paradise right here in West Seattle," beams instructor and owner Marybeth Spector. "I really feel blessed to be given the chance to be a steward of this land."

> ## "It's a little piece of paradise right here in West Seattle."
>
> Marybeth Spector
> instructor

Spector is a third-generation West Seattleite with the maiden name of Armitstead, for all you long-time locals who may know her family. She attended Madison Middle School and graduated from West Seattle High—a true native through and through.

A dancer who traveled the world, Spector discovered yoga in 1963 and began taking her practice on the road with her wherever she went. She came back to Seattle in 1975, read stacks of yoga books while continuing to practice, and finally discovered her teacher Chris Dormaier in West Seattle in 1997.

"I began to study and do teacher training with Chris three years ago at West Seattle's own Sound Yoga," explains Spector. "I also began teaching on my own and then opened up my front room studio."

Yoga For Our Times is a one-woman show featuring two weekly classes, private weekend classes, and enriching group retreats (green thumbs rejoice as these retreats are tailor-made for gardeners).

On a typical retreat, or a "3-hour vacation" as Spector calls it, students start with a practice that teaches postures to help ready the body for gardening. Then the group takes a break to discuss gardening, from elaborate grounds to pots on the porch, however vast their interest happens to be. Next, Spector takes the students through a restorative practice with five to six postures to rest and stretch the body after gardening. The finale features a walk in the garden to reflect on stillness followed by tea in the lovely gazebo.

These are general classes for all levels and abilities. "This is perfect as a beginner's class if ever there was one," encourages Spector. "It's very gentle. No standing on your elbows, I promise!"

Retreats are popular group escapes for birthdays, bridal showers, family gatherings, and office getaways. Drop some hints and maybe your boss will spring for a yoga-filled morale booster. You can almost smell the blooming clematis now.

A lush garden, gentle yoga, and a supportive instructor. What more could you need? Perhaps just a taxicab to take your loose-limbed self back home!

What:
Yoga in the Garden

Where:
Yoga For Our Times
3350 58th Ave SW
www.yogaforourtimes.com
206.938.3381

When:
General classes:
Tuesday & Thursday at 8:30 am

Private classes and retreats:
Saturday & Sunday

Price:
Individual classes $12
Six class card $60
Private 1.5–hour class $65
Retreats $65

85 | Walker Rock Garden

Looking for a unique way to spend an afternoon outdoors with friends or family? Get some solid points for creativity when you visit Walker Rock Garden.

Located on 37th Aveune SW in the back yard of the Walker family residence, Walker Rock Garden is a mecca for geologists and a pleasurable art walk for the average visitor.

Managed by Sandy Adams, daughter of the late Milton and Florence Walker, the rock-themed backyard park was lovingly created by her father and nurtured by her mother for more than 20 years.

> *"He [Walker] would dress up as a tourist and walk around and listen to what people had to say about his art."*
>
> Sandy Adams
> manager

"Mom did the garden work and Dad built the rock sculptures," says Adams.

Milton Walker was a Boeing employee with an artistic side that flourished in the medium of stones, pebbles, and boulders.

"He was the little guy that crawled way into the wing of the plane and worked on intricate tube bending," she recalls. "He was wiry and always very active."

Walker began building his rock garden after his youngest son joined the military. He spent the next two decades spontaneously cultivating his passion.

"Dad didn't draw up a plan. He'd just go out there and create," Adams reflects.

Once, her father scored a large pile of his building material—10 tons, in fact—on a trip to Oregon when he met a man selling his rock collection for a mere $150.

ENRICHMENT

"He picked them up in his Dodge Dart and U-Haul trailer, came home, and unloaded them all in the driveway," she laughs, remembering.

With all those rocks, Walker had quite a task ahead of him. He spent hours outside in the yard creating. And in the winter, when the weather was not so welcoming, Walker would stay indoors and sort rocks by size and color.

He continued to build until late in life. In fact, at age 70, Walker and his wife put up an 18-foot tower you will notice driving by. And people of all ages can still enjoy their creations today.

"The rock garden is a work of art. Not a playground, but rather a garden for adults," says Adams. "Schoolkids enjoy it when they come, but adults can more fully appreciate what went into it."

According to Adams, her father had a tremendous sense of humor and loved to overhear comments from visiting critics.

"On Mother's Day he always knew there would be a lot of people here, so he would dress up as a tourist and walk around and listen to what people had to say about his art," she says.

What:
Walker Rock Garden

Where:
5407 37th Ave SW
The family has asked us not to publish the phone number, but you can access it by looking in the residential phone listings under the name "Walker Rock Garden."

When:
Year-round, but spring and summer are ideal

Price:
Free

"The one comment I remember most was when a fourth grade student said, 'I think this is what heaven must be like,'" she smiles. "They have never seen anything like it!"

What are the odds of encountering a piece of West Seattle history and a child's picture of paradise at the same time? Just visit the Walker Rock Garden. It's only a stone's throw away.

86 | Massage with a View on Alki

If the sound of West Seattle's waves and the feeling of sand between your toes is not a soothing enough environment for you, how about a massage? Or even better, a massage with a view.

Stroll up the stairs to Alki View Massage (just above Homefront Smoothies) and feel your stress wash its way out to sea.

The converted beach bungalow features three rooms with Puget Sound views and a beachy, neighborhood feel you simply won't find at your typical spa. Rather than the standard Zen-themed décor, you have palm trees, bamboo, and a view of the water. And instead of the recorded nature sound CDs played at most spas, Alki View offers the real deal—gentle breezes, seagulls, waves, and all.

Founded by Jessica and Michelle DeShayes, twins born and raised in Burien, Alki View Massage has been a long-standing dream. Jessica remembers scribbling in her journal years ago that her goal was to "do massages on Alki."

> *"People love that we are twins—we produce a radiant amount of energy together."*
>
> Jessica DeShayes
> massage therapist and co-owner

The DeShayes sisters graduated from the Brenneke School of Massage in 1997. Since graduation they have both managed their own chair massage and full-body accounts, worked in chiropractics, and opened Alki View.

Let the gals give you true beach treatment, including everything from traditional Swedish massage to hot stone, paraffin, or deep tissue massages.

"In addition to those here for relaxation, I have worked on everything from clients with MS and those suffering from fibromyalgia to severe car accidents," explains Jessica. "Due to our chiropractic background, our specialty is definitely treatment."

Guests are also delighted and entertained that they can double their

ENRICHMENT

pleasure because the sister therapists are twins.

"They love that we are twins—we produce a radiant amount of energy together," smiles Jessica.

The two have decided to run with this idea and have even created a special "Twin Tandem" massage to showcase their natural-born talents.

Another stimulating difference between Alki View and other West Seattle Spas is the sweet sensation of the Chocolate, Raspberry, and Cognac Nectar massage. But the stand-out distinction is the view. The beach community and visitors alike have embraced this new seaside haven for relaxation.

"People say they really love our location," smiles Jessica. "They say that there is nothing like this down here and that it's just what the beach needed."

Even as sportbikes and convertibles whiz by, the DeShayes sisters will take you on a relaxing journey to the more tranquil side of Alki. Just head up to their retreat for a break from the scene without leaving the scenery.

What:
Alki View Massage

Where:
5963 SW Carroll St.
www.alkiviewmassage.com
206.387.3944

When:
Open daily; call for appointments
Walk-ins also welcome

Prices:
Treatments vary; please
call for prices

87 | Discover the Art of Glass Blowing

There's something cooking in West Seattle. Professional artists and students alike are flocking to it. Shoppers, retailers, and gallery-goers are buying it. Some even claim the act itself is addictive.

It's the fascinating and fire-hot art of glass blowing.

Visit the Icon Grill or flip on a PBS special about Dale Chihuly, and you'll see that Seattle is a mecca for this medium. Now, for more than a decade, West Seattle has been home to two full-blown (pun intended) studios. And word on the street is, many local artists are also creating this molten magic out of their garages.

> *"It's beautiful when it's cold as a finished piece, but when it's hot, it's amazing."*
>
> Matt Hooks
> Lagarto Glass owner

Stroll by the studios at Avalon Glassworks or Lagarto Glass on Pigeon Point and you'll witness the orange glow of molten glass metamorphosing into vibrant vases, garden floats, and brilliantly colored works of art.

"We're just doing our part to help Seattle continue to be a center for glass blowing," smiles Shannon Felix, who co-owns of Avalon Glassworks with her husband. Jon Felix previously worked as a chemist making glass for industrial use. Now he and his wife run Avalon's art gallery and gift shop and hire some of Seattle's best in the field to produce studio line work. While Avalon does offer private lessons and studio rental, they are more set up for professional artists who already know how to blow.

Lagarto Glass, however, features a wide range of classes such as glass blowing, casting, bead-making, fusing, etching, and stained glass creation. The classes are offered through several different institutions, including University of Washington Experimental College, South Seattle Community College, and Discover U (check each school's website for more info). For the novice to the expert, these classes educate students on the entire process of glass-making over a length of time. Lagarto also does private lessons for any level.

West Seattle native and owner of Lagarto Glass, Matt Hooks has been working with glass art for over 20 years. He began blowing glass in 1990 and has been teaching the art since 1997.

"I've devoted my life to glass," nods Hooks. "I'm like a total sponge when it comes to my passion. In fact, me and my friends in the industry call ourselves 'glass nerds.'"

Even in the heat of his hot shop on a humid summer afternoon, Hooks' eyes light up just mentioning the G-word. Pointing to a recently completed pair of brilliant blue glass fish, he reflects: "It's beautiful when it's cold as a finished piece, but when it's hot, it's amazing."

Hooks tells first-timers to beware— not of the heat but of the habit-forming effect of glass blowing.

"Once it's in your blood, watch out," he cautions.

For a perfect pastime for out-of-town guests, have them take a private lesson at Lagarto. Or if they'd rather just watch, swing by Avalon to witness the fiery display. In-house glass blowers are happy to interact with the public and answer questions. And they also sell beautiful "souvenirs" in the gallery.

If you haven't seen this amazing art in the making before, jump on it. Chances are it will blow your mind.

What:
Glass Blowing

Where:
Avalon Glassworks
2914 SW Avalon Way
www.avalonglassworks.com
206.937.6369

Lagarto Glass
1904 SW Dawson St.
www.LagartoGlass.net
206.762.7148

When:
Avalon Glassworks
Monday–Friday 10 am–6 pm
Saturday & Sunday 10 am–5 pm

Lagarto Glass gallery hours
Monday–Friday 9 am–5 pm
Saturday Noon–4 pm

See class schedules at:
www.discoveru.org
www.southseattle.edu
www.experimental.asuw.org

Price:
Prices vary; call or see websites

88 | Tai Chi on the Beach

Relax. Breathe in. And move to improve your body and your mind. Introducing "Tai Chi on the Beach." A gentle Chinese movement exercise, Tai Chi is nothing new to martial arts, or to West Seattle for that matter, but the class on the waterfront has intrigued participants and passersby for years.

"We offer it free for people who don't have time to make it to regular scheduled classes," says chief instructor, or as they say in the biz "Sifu," Restita DeJesus. "That way anyone can gain the benefits of Tai Chi's relaxation and stress relief."

> "It's a gentle exercise that anyone can do, and it keeps people fit and happy."
>
> Restita DeJesus
> Sifu (teacher)

Co-founder of the Yin Yang Arts Center in West Seattle, Sifu DeJesus has taught martial arts since 1982 and Tai Chi since 1996. She is a certified instructor of Tai Chi under Master Yijiao Hong and a continuing Tai Chi champion at both national and international levels.

A West Seattle weekend morning tradition for years, "Tai Chi on the Beach" class begins flowing at 8 a.m. every Saturday from May until late September.

"It started as a fun outing for our regular class," explains DeJesus. "We'd say, 'let's go to the beach this time,' and it grew from there."

Now, this moving mass of meditation is its own entity.

Located at Don Armeni Park, the class offers one of the best city views imaginable. But with Tai Chi, students are a world away from the hustle and bustle.

An ancient art, Tai Chi can be described as "seeking harmony through movement." It focuses on the philosophy of "yin and yang," universal opposites that constantly seek to balance and harmonize. Though Tai

Chi started out with a fighting aspect, you won't see any Bruce Lee action on Alki.

Commonly called "moving meditation," Tai Chi is different from other martial arts such as karate or kung fu in that it is focused from the inside out.

"We concentrate on inner strength as opposed to just physical strength," says DeJesus. But the art also offers physical benefits.

The practice of slow, flowing movements is known to effectively strengthen muscles, increase balance, improve posture, and decrease blood pressure. It also has therapeutic qualities such as relief from hypertension and anxiety and can even help with rehabilitation after major surgeries.

"I have one student that started class with emphysema and with Tai Chi has increased his lung capacity," remarks DeJesus.

Tai Chi is an exercise accessible for all ages and body conditions. According to DeJesus, even students in wheelchairs or those without use of major body regions can still practice movement, flow, and breathing. It's open to all—from seniors and teens to unsuspecting passersby.

What:
Tai Chi on the Beach

Where:
Don Armeni Park on Harbor Avenue
www.yyac.com
206.935.2315

When:
Saturday 8–9 am
May–September

Price:
Free

"We have a core of returning students each year, but we see new people all the time," she says. "Some people walk by and observe, but there are spontaneous people who see us and jump right in.

"It's a gentle exercise that anyone can do, and it keeps people fit and happy," smiles DeJesus.

Looking for a graceful mixture of movement and meditation? There's a spot on the lawn just waiting for you.

89 | Train for TRI on Westside Terrain

Steep, treacherous hills. Long, scenic flats. Surrounded on three sides by water with a handful of pools to boot, West Seattle's an ideal neighborhood to train for a triathlon.

> There is no shortage of road rides on the Westside.

Whether you take advantage of this versatile little peninsula for swimming, riding, or running, it has everything you need to do all three.

Swimming

Though the waters surrounding West Seattle prove too chilly for most, many hardcore triathletes don a good wetsuit and practice swimming in the tough conditions of the open water. Want to stick to saltwater but avoid hypothermia and harbor seals? Colman Pool, a saltwater wonder in Lincoln Park, is open from Memorial Day through Labor Day for summertime training. A few good indoor locations for year-round swimming include the Southwest Community Pool, the YMCA, and Allstar Fitness. The latter two require membership.

Biking

There is no shortage of road rides on the Westside. Practice spinning on the flats of Alki Avenue to get your speed up and consider hooking up with the Duwamish Trail to get in longer distances (grab a bike trail map at Alki Bike & Board to scope out a good route). Then begin to work your way up in terms of hill difficulty. Many start by tackling Avalon and move on to Admiral Way, the north end of California, Marine View Drive, and even Charlestown! Any way you look at it, conquering West Seattle's steep terrain will get you that much closer to mastering a challenging, hilly triathlon course.

Running

The only question about running in West Seattle is, where to begin? Many simply start at the doorstep. Similar to course training for road biking, running for triathlon training requires both hills and flats. The Alki/Harbor Avenue course provides flat, night-lit, mile-marked paved trails and stunning views of downtown and the Olympic Mountains. For those who prefer dirt trails to pavement, Lincoln Park during daylight hours is hard to beat. For good hill climbs, follow well-lit arterials such as both sides of Admiral Way, Avalon, and 35th Avenue. The easiest of the three sports to "get out the door quick and do" and requiring very little gear, running is recommended anywhere in West Seattle as long as you look both ways and watch your step.

So, whether you're preparing for a sprint triathlon, like the popular Danskin TRI, or you're bound and determined to be an Ironman on Maui, get started right here. West Seattle terrain—a prime place to train.

What:
Train for a Triathlon

Where:
Westside Terrain

When:
Year-round, depending on whether you swim in the Sound

Price:
Free, plus equipment

90 | Take the Homes with History Tour

Nearly every spring in West Seattle, doors to the past open for intrigued visitors. Wooden banisters creak and antique chandeliers shine as area history is revealed and personal curiosities are filled. Finally there's a chance to see what lies inside that beautiful old home down the street with the Southwest Seattle Historical Society's Homes with History Tour.

A self-guided discovery of community history, the tour occurs in May and features a handful of historic homes, all built before 1940.

"Many of the homes on the tour are older than the people walking through them," says local historian Clay Eals.

Eals helped originate the tour in 1989, inspired by the buzz of Washington State's Centennial.

"The centennial was being promoted all over the state, and individual historical societies were encouraged to come up with events to coincide with it," he recalls. "So we created the tour, among other things, and it went so well we've been doing it almost every year since."

> "Many of the homes on the tour are older than the people walking through them."
>
> Clay Eals
> local historian

The tour itself is a fairly monumental undertaking, both logistically and historically, using between 70 and 100 volunteers annually to expose the community to yesteryear.

"We strive to educate people about the heritage of this area," says Eals. "It's part of our mission to develop great community pride, establish stronger roots in the neighborhood, and help people appreciate the past to better approach our future."

ENRICHMENT

The *West Seattle Herald* usually publishes an insert for the tour with maps, photos, and info about each home. You can see as few or as many as you like within event hours. Some come by car, while others bike or walk. Volunteers wait at the door to greet you (and make sure you remove your shoes before entering).

How are homes selected for the tour?

"It's an interesting process," says committee chair Joey Richesson. "We have knocked on the doors of great historical houses, and at the same time, individual homeowners have called and asked to participate."

"These homeowners are true heroes," says Eals. "They voluntarily maintain and preserve these one-of-a-kind structures and then open them up for the public to see."

For participating in the tour, each homeowner receives a bouquet of flowers to display, a historic write-up, and a plaque donated by Northwest Art & Frame that features a "now" photo and a corresponding "then" (1938) photo of the home from the Puget Sound regional branch of the state archive.

What:
Homes with History Tour

Where:
Tour changes yearly; contact the Log House Museum
www.loghousemuseum.org
206.938.5293

When:
The month of May (call or visit website for dates)

Price:
Advance tickets $15
Tickets at the door $20

Eals notes that the neighborhood has a whole lot to see. "West Seattle really has some jewels to show off."

"During the tour we hear a lot of people say they either grew up next door, live on the block, or that they've 'always loved this house' and are curious what it looks like inside," Richesson says with a laugh. "Who doesn't love going into somebody else's home and taking a look?"

91 | Intense Alternative at X Gym

Ever noticed the SUV driving around West Seattle that reads "X Gym: 20 minutes 2 X a week" and wondered, "What's that all about?"

Sharmon and P.J. Glassey, X Gym president and CEO respectively, can give you the low-down on how they pump you up.

"Traditional weight training requires one hour, three times per week," reflects P.J. Glassey. "People don't have time for that these days."

> *"In 20 minutes every major muscle group gets a workout equivalent to about 2 to 4 hours of conventional training."*
>
> P.J. Glassey
> X Gym CEO

A high-intensity workout style designed for busy people trying to be more efficient while keeping in top shape, the X Gym claims to take only 20 minutes twice a week.

"In 20 minutes every major muscle group gets a workout equivalent to about 2 to 4 hours of conventional training," nods Glassey.

According to X Gym trainers, their one-on-one personal training program typically produces triple the results of traditional methods in less than one-third of the time commitment.

Sounds great. But it seems counterintuitive. How do you decrease workout time, reduce frequency, and increase results?

The answer lies in the level of intensity, according to X Gym. Traditional workout methods (weight training with sets and reps) were established by Eugene Sandow in 1891. But X Gym disagrees with this century-old technique.

"It's ballistic in nature," Glassey explains. "Using heavy weights and fast reps, people get discouraged with their workout, not to mention injured."

The X Gym's MO is a workout with lighter weights, fewer reps, and higher-intensity training.

"We all know the guy at Gold's Gym who can outlift everyone on his favorite machine," smiles Glassey. "But take him hiking, for example, and he can't keep up."

Which is exactly what the X Gym strives to combat with functional strength and endurance training. Trainers say their clients increase muscular strength without bulking up.

"They get strong and toned, and increase their endurance," explains Glassey.

Keeping on the cutting edge of fitness studies, the X Gym credits its research to health journals such as *Physician's Sports Medicine Magazine* and to the National Strength and Conditioning Association.

The staff has designed seven exclusive "exercise protocols," whereas traditional practices use only one method. Each X Gym method lasts seven weeks emphasizing a different muscle-fiber type and energy system.

"We change methods often because research says after six to seven weeks the mind gets tired of routine," explains Glassey. "So we change it up to keep the neurological, biological, and muscular systems in a constant state of progress."

X Gym President, Sharmon Glassey, also points out that the X Gym is not only meant for getting in shape but is also designed to help with recovery from injury, sickness, and other health-related issues.

What:
The X Gym

Where:
3213 Harbor Ave
www.xgym.com
206.938.9496

When:
See website for gym hours

Price:
$245 per month

"Part of our job is to take poor-health issues and turn them into success," she says. "In fact, I'd say the majority of my clients have trained at the X Gym to help them fight cancer, diabetes, and obesity."

Looking for a new, non-traditional work out this year? Then get intense (for 20 minutes at a time, at least) at the X Gym.

92 | Tae Kwon Do with the Kids

Time is precious, but so is family. As is getting daily exercise. And, well, everything else. If you want to kick the habit of overextending, consider making exercise efficiency your top priority.

Instead of dropping off the kids at karate class and picking them up later, neglecting your own workout in the meantime, try practicing tae kwon do together at Lee's Martial Arts.

> "We really believe in bringing the community together by offering a class that teaches respect, self defense, and discipline for kids and adults."
>
> Lisa Skvarla
> instructor

Growing in popularity (as well as practicality), parent-child tae kwon do classes at Lee's allow you to spend more time hanging out with your kids, and getting your exercise and less time driving around town wishing you had more time.

But parents, be warned: This is not a spectator sport. No sitting on the sidelines allowed. In this class, parents and children are equal participants. The two groups do separate during certain points of the class to hone their skills independently, but they share all the benefits—increased strength, better balance, and more flexibility.

"The martial arts provide a year-round activity that truly complements all other sports as well as a healthy state of mind," explains instructor Lisa Skvarla. "And keeping true to the class name, the instruction is actually taught by both kids and adults."

Lisa and husband Joe Skvarla teach the class along with their kids, Kathryn and Stephen. Lisa is a black belt and personal trainer, Joe is a black belt, Stephen is an orange belt, and Kathryn received first place in the forms division at the Washington State Open. Each member has been trained under the supervision of Master Tae S. Lee. The strength of the family unit could never be more apparent (figuratively and physically).

"We really believe in bringing the community together by offering a class that teaches respect, self-defense, and discipline for kids and adults," says Skvarla.

Inspired by child and adult students alike, the class is the first of its kind for Lee's Martial Arts and a relatively new concept for active West Seattle families. But there's also more on offer at Lee's, including cardio boot kick camp as well as a women's self defense class.

So grab your kids and step up to the mat at Lee's Martial Arts. Because according to Skvarla, a family that kicks together sticks together.

What:
Parent-Child
Tae Kwon Do Class

Where:
Lee's Martial Arts
3270 California Ave SW
www.lees-martialarts.com
206.938.3375
206.935.6000

When:
Tuesday & Thursday
5:30–6:30 pm

Price:
Two times per week is
$140/mo; once a week is
$70/mo (price includes
entire family)

93 | *West Seattle's School of Fish*

Something fishy's going on in the Alaska Junction: a seafood market opening its doors while opening the minds of West Seattleites to fascinating fish knowledge.

Seattle Fish Co. is not just seafood retail, but what you might call the neighborhood's own "school of fish." It's not seeking the status of a Westside Pike Place nor an over-the-top gourmet grocery, but instead hopes to be a place that explores the depths of fish facts and truly teaches the customer.

> *"Our philosophy is to give people information and ideas, so they walk away knowing more than they did when they came in the door."*
>
> Hobey Grote
> owner

"We're not hustling fish here," says owner Hobey Grote. "We are a fish market that provides an experience and, more importantly, an education."

So, no low-flying fish here. You might, however, learn something. At least that's the goal of Grote and retail manager Bill Liston.

"Our philosophy is to give people information and ideas, so they walk away knowing more than they did when they came in the door," nods Grote. "We want them to know where the fish comes from, how it is caught, how it should be handled, what it tastes like, and how to prepare it."

Name a fish and Liston will rattle off almost anything you'd want to know about it, including an arsenal of great recipe ideas.

With long-standing industry experience, the two men are a salty set of fish fanatics with a plan to tutor the neighborhood. Being surrounded by water on three sides, Westside residents seem receptive.

"We've seen over 100 people here on any given day," smiles Grote.

So why did Grote choose West Seattle? Besides residing here, he felt the neighborhood was under-served. "There was no full-service fish market here, so what we are doing is offering 60 to 70 products to choose from every single day."

With this range of seafood options, you'll find fish here you might not normally encounter at your grocery store.

"I go to the airport every day to make sure it's as fresh as possible," describes Grote. "And I order a little bit of everything to help introduce new fish to people."

Seattle Fish Co. entices customers with preparation ideas and products to broaden their cooking comfort zone. Available selections include anything from octopus to South Pacific snapper.

"With seafood, often people go with what they know and new things can be somewhat intimidating," explains manager Courtney Grote. "What we're trying to do is demystify the less commonly known fish and encourage people to try something new."

Seattle Fish Co. offers cooking classes and wine tastings in their small seafood-related grocery (featuring local goods). They also supply fish to many area restaurants such as Ovio Bistro, Café Zaffarano, and Celtic Swell. And if you want to share your Seattle fish bounty with relatives back East, Seattle Fish Co. also offers fish shipping online—fresh from the docks to the front door.

Whatever you're craving—halibut, wild coho, or exotic opah—learn something new each time you visit West Seattle's very own School of Fish.

What:
Fish Education

Where:
Seattle Fish Co.
4435 California Ave SW
www.fromthedocks.com
206.938.7576

When:
Daily 10 am–7:30 pm

Price:
Prices vary by the pound, inquire within

94 | *Oriental Medicine Opens Door for Injured*

Have an annoying sports injury that won't go away? Need to loosen up stiff muscles? Or, does the stress of a go-go-go lifestyle simply put you on pins and needles? If so, maybe that's exactly what you need.

Introducing West Seattle Acupuncture & Oriental Medicine—where Paul G. Nojaim L.Ac. sets your body and mind at ease.

Before you begin, Nojaim checks in and helps you "listen" to your body.

> *"When your body hurts, it is trying to tell you that something is wrong, that some change needs to happen to find a healthier balance."*
>
> Paul G. Nojaim
> acupuncturist

"When your body hurts, it is trying to tell you that something is wrong, that some change needs to happen to find a healthier balance," he states.

Take for example ex-BMX pro Scott Matual. A bike racer for more than 20 years, Matual is a passionate cyclist who wants to continue riding for life. But at age 35, Matual is already feeling debilitating effects from years of competition.

"I used to race and still ride road, downhill, and mountain bikes aggressively," he explains while rubbing his neck. "But my neck and back always bother me after I ride, and I'm developing arthritis in my right hand—my rear brake hand."

Turned on to acupuncture by a cyclist friend, Matual was advised to have a combination treatment—acupuncture and cupping therapy.

Acupuncture pierces specific body areas with fine needles to relieve pain. Cupping uses glass jars and a flame to create suction on the skin, thereby increasing blood flow for a sensation similar to a deep tissue massage.

ENRICHMENT

As Nojaim puts stainless steel needles into place on the patient's body, he explains, "In Chinese medicine there's a notion of 'qi.' When we have pain, that means our qi gets stuck. So I am loosening up those areas to get things flowing."

But anyone who's never tried it asks, 'Does it hurt?" In general, the answer is no, but sometimes there's a bit of a stinging sensation. When the needling is done, Nojaim leaves the room, allowing the patient to rest while the treatment takes effect. He returns several minutes later. Then cupping begins.

"I apply little vacuum jars onto the back and use a flame to suck the skin up and get the blood moving," Nojaim explains.

"It feels like an octopus has a hold of me," laughs Matual. "But it feels good."

After treatment, the patient tends to feel sleepy in the short-term then relieved from pain for weeks. Two days after treatment, Matual said his back felt better than it had in years. The only side effects are strange purple circles left by the cupping jars that last about a week. But according to most, it's a small price to pay for feeling better.

What:
Oriental Medicine

Where:
West Seattle Acupuncture & Oriental Medicine
5410 California Ave SW
206.923.2053

When:
Monday–Saturday
9 am–7 pm

Price:
Treatments vary in price; call to inquire

"There's a physical and mental aspect to injury, and you can't treat one without the other. But once you start, you begin to find a balance that changes everyone for the better," says Nojaim.

If Scott Matual is any proof, there's something to be said for the 4000-year-old Chinese practice. To experience these Far Eastern benefits for yourself right here and now in West Seattle, visit West Seattle Acupuncture.

95 | Sit Back and Bee Wax

Sit down in a room of butter-yellow, art-laden walls. Breathe in the scent of "burning harmony" candles and beeswax. Tip back your cup of freshly-brewed herbal tea, and you'll see that Bee Waxed is a fine way to relax in West Seattle.

Sip your tea in the honeycomb-like refuge of the lobby.

Located on 35th Avenue SW in the small retail hub next to Casablanca Coffee, Bee Waxed Spa opened its doors in 2003. The space is rumored to have been a cowboy gear store back in the early 1900s, and still holds its mystique today.

Sip your tea in the honeycomb-like refuge of a lobby and then head back to the treatment room where you can choose between a variety of facials or—you guessed it—waxing.

"Some people have asked me why I don't do nails and other services," explains Bee Waxed Spa owner and esthetician Bren Sullivan. "But I wanted to focus on just two treatments and do them very well."

Sullivan spent years performing these very treatments both at La Serenity Spa in Bellevue and Wax On Spa in Belltown. She's a skin care specialist you may also recognize from her days at the Nordstrom's Clinique make-up counter downtown.

But Sullivan began beeswaxing for many reasons.

"I felt like I already ran the business downtown, so I knew how to do it," she reflects. "But I also wanted clients to be treated a certain way, in a better way, and I could do that on my own."

In addition to offering waxing and facials, Sullivan also features her art, which she creates in the workshop behind the treatment room—making her new space serve a dual purpose.

"I'm an artist, so I wanted a place where I could not only work on my art during my days off from the spa, but also somewhere I could display the work in more of a gallery-like setting," she explains.

Gracing the spa walls, Sullivan's art includes mixed-media tile work, paintings, drawings, and sculpture. In fact, a piece behind her reception desk sold within her first week of operation.

Bee Waxed has quickly become a busy biz. While she advises calling ahead to make an appointment, Sullivan is pleasantly surprised at the walk-in business as well.

"I have seen a surprising amount of men!" she smiles.

While waxing is big with the fellows, Sullivan also offers them a few special facials such as the Men's Exclusive Facial and the popular Men's Sport Facial.

"These facials really introduce men to the world of skin care," she nods.

Bee Waxed also features lash tinting, glycolic peels, mini facials, 1-hour luxury facials (including deep cleansing, toning, exfoliation, extraction, massage, custom masque, and moisturizing) as well as waxing for, well, pretty much any area you wish.

So buzz on by and give it a try when you're in the neighborhood. As soon as you step inside, you'll find it easy just sit back and bee wax.

What:
Bee Waxed Spa

Where:
7352 35th Ave SW
www.beewaxedspa.com
206.938.5177

When:
Tuesday-Saturday
10 am–7 pm

Price:
See website as treatments vary

96 | Hot Yoga on the Westside

As you walk by, the vibrant flame-painted studio makes you wonder, "What's going on in there…art? Exercise?" You can try to sneak a peak through the window, but you'll get just a tiny taste of what's inside.

To truly understand the happenings at 4747 California, you simply have to open the door, lie on the floor in a well-heated room with fans spinning above, and let the soothing sound of your instructor's voice bring you through the moving meditation that is Bikram "hot" yoga.

Said to be one of the more challenging beginning yoga classes, this 90-minute posture flow was created by Bikram Choudhury. Conducted in a very warm room, the course features breathing exercises and 26 Hatha yoga postures repeated twice in sequence.

Yoga, okay. But, why the heat?

"Practicing in a well-heated room helps us stretch—it aids flexibility, helps avoid injury by 'pre-heating' muscles, and aids in detoxification," explains director Amber Borgomainerio.

> **"The body changes and shifts. It lightens up; it loosens up—you lose the things in life that weigh you down, whether it be weight, stress, scar tissue or emotional tensions."**
>
> Amber Borgomainerio
> director

Borgomainerio was trained by Bikram himself at his international headquarters in L.A. The West Seattleite had to complete a rigorous 2-month, 500-hour intensive training program to become certified to teach and has been doing so ever since.

"Once you establish a practice for yourself, the body changes and shifts. It lightens up, it loosens up—you lose the things in life that weigh you down, whether it be weight, stress, scar tissue, or emotional tensions."

Meaning 'union' in Sanskrit, yoga connects body, mind, and soul, and improves the health between them. Where better physical health is a result of frequent practice, improved mental health is often an unexpected benefit. For example, one student initially began to rehab her hip, but now that it's healed, she's decided to continue practicing for all the other benefits.

"Bikram yoga is a very transforming experience," says studio owner Neil Cooper.

"It works with each system of the body," explains Borgomainerio. "Each posture leads to the next, systematically working the whole body from the inside out, from the muscular and skeletal systems to the immune and nervous system."

Much of the "magic" behind this practice is due to the "tourniquet" effect, meaning it stretches, squeezes, and massages internal organs and tissues, while flushing out toxins and improving circulation.

"[It's] an isometric exercise—as you stretch one part of the body, you strengthen another," says Borgomainerio.

So people all over West Seattle are posing like never before. "We are building a yoga community that has grown to be very strong," says Cooper.

"It's a place where you can take a break from life and get your body healthy in every aspect," beams Borgomainerio.

Cooper agrees and points to students who have grown because of Bikram as proof.

"It's touched a lot of people," he smiles. "It's really rewarding to know it's helping people better deal with things like injuries, cancer, divorce, job loss, or just being stressed out."

So if you're feeling the heat of life's everyday dilemmas, try breaking a sweat for a more positive purpose with Bikram Hot Yoga.

What:
Bikram Hot Yoga

Where:
4747 California Ave.
206.937.3900

When:
Mon–Fri 9:30 am, 4:30 & 6:30 pm
Tuesday & Thursday 7 am
Saturday & Sunday 9 am & 5 pm
Power Vinyasa classes are also offered, call for schedule

Price:
One-time drop-in visits run $15, but prices and packages vary

97 | Get Growing at the P-Patch

There's something growing behind the tennis courts on Fauntleroy Way.

Pull in the parking lot on Webster and look up at the big grass-covered hill. You'll see a brilliant array of cosmos, marigolds, and zinnias among pumpkins, red corn, and giant sunflowers. You'll also notice the sunshiny smiles on nearly every gardener tending a plot.

Welcome to West Seattle's Solstice Park P-Patch.

The Solstice Park P-Patch is a place to plant your own plot and grow in more ways than one. People can become more in touch with both earth and environment while making positive use of the land and their time.

> *"It's fun to share the homegrown foods with friends and neighbors and to create your meals around what you grow in your p-patch plot."*
>
> Barbara Olson
> volunteer and plot leaser

"More and more younger people are becoming involved," says Barbara Olson, a p-patch construction volunteer, plot leaser, and avid gardener. "You learn by doing. Anybody can start anywhere. It's a very educational experience."

Olson, who lives in a condominium, became a Seattle p-patch supporter when she wanted to teach her grandson the art of gardening but had no garden to grow in. Now she shares a plot at Solstice Park P-Patch where she nurtures and grows everything from potatoes and red cabbage to tomatoes and gooseberry bushes.

"It's fun to share the homegrown foods with friends and neighbors and to create your meals around what you grow in your p-patch plot," she says.

But these yummy fruits and veggies didn't just sprout up on their own. The Solstice Park P-Patch has been slowly growing in community members' minds for quite some time.

The planning for the p-patch began in 1999, and the first fruits of everyone's labor were harvested the fall of 2004.

"Constructing the plots was hard work," recalls Marja van Pietersom, former volunteer coordinator and project manager. "We had to dig out giant boulders and everything."

The site now features 40 plots with an ever-expanding waiting list of anxious plot-pursuers.

"I think it's a real plus for the neighborhood," smiles Olson. "There's more landscaping, it's fun to walk through, and it's always a pleasure to see a garden."

"For most of us, the construction of Solstice Park P-Patch has created a real bond with people in the neighborhood," says van Pietersom.

What:
Solstice Park P-Patch

Where:
On the corner of Webster and Fauntleroy (behind the tennis courts)

For questions or to sign up for a plot, visit or call:
The Department of Neighborhoods
700 3rd Ave 4th Floor
www.seattle.gov/
neighborhoods/ppatch
206.684.0264

When:
Year-round

Price:
Free to wander; call to find out plot prices

Like an outdoor community center, Solstice Park P-Patch not only provides a welcoming neighborhood place to visit, but it also offers a chance for people to meet one another—a chance to build community.

"It a great project," says van Pietersom. "It took an enormous amount of time and energy but everybody's very proud of the gardens and the addition it's made to the neighborhood."

Want to take root in your community while reaping the benefits of homegrown goodness? Swing on by the p-patch and get things growing.

98 | Surprise Yourself at Toastmasters

Every first and third Tuesday of the month something surprising happens in West Seattle. Stand outside the meeting room doors at a local club and you'll hear applause. Then laughter. Then more applause.

Whatever is going on in there sounds like a whole lot of fun. And according to members of West Seattle Toastmasters Club 832, it is.

"Most people show up for their first West Seattle Toastmasters Club 832 meeting with some degree of trepidation," says member and advertising professional Bruce Bulloch. "They see their public speaking abilities as a barrier to their professional and personal goals, so Toastmasters finds its way onto the New Year's resolutions list and finally, reluctantly, is translated into action."

But that action provides unanticipated results.

Application and costs range from $24 to $39 per year depending on the month you join.

"What they don't expect is to have fun," smiles Bulloch. "Surprise seems to be the typical reaction of guests at their first meeting."

Bulloch became involved in the organization in order to improve his speaking abilities in ad presentations. He was surprised by the ability and expertise of some of the West Seattle speakers as well as their intention to have fun.

"This is a group of people that is serious about improving speaking skills but is not about to make the mistake of taking themselves too seriously," says Bulloch. "There's an infectious sense of humor that permeates the meetings as well as a real sense of camaraderie."

New members are also surprised by how supportive the club is no matter how inexperienced the speaker might be. "Everyone is pulling for you, eager to show support," says Bulloch.

A typical night consists of three speeches and an evaluation of each followed by impromptu speeches and joke-telling—all run by the "Toastmaster," or the master of ceremonies. Guests are always welcome to come by and see what it's all about.

Toastmasters has a formal curriculum that is followed by each member. New members are led through a series of speaking exercises that touch on different aspects of the public-speaking skill set, from speech organization to vocal variety to use of visual aids.

After a number of months, members often step back and take a look at the progress they've made.

"Newer members realize they project a much different image in front of an audience than they did when they first came," says Bulloch.

They develop a level of skill and confidence that they didn't think was possible before walking in. So if you're standing outside, listening to the laughs and wondering if this is for you, try opening that door as well as your mind to the opportunity. You might be surprised with what you find.

What:
Talk It up at Toastmasters

Where:
3000 California Ave SW
www.westseattletm832.org

When:
6:30–8 pm
1st & 3rd Tues of the month
Guests welcome

Price:
$24–$39 yearly, depending
on when you join

99 | A Wild Way to Heal

Walk up the stairs and you'll know almost instantly that you are in for a wild experience. First, you'll be greeted by four cats and a curious dog named Puma. Then, depending on whether you arrive solo or with your pet, you'll hop on the table or the couch for your session.

Introducing Wild Reiki & Shamanic Healing by Rose De Dan.

An alternative type of healing for pets and people, De Dan's practice blends Reiki, shamanic healing, and Acutonics® to treat everything from animal arthritis to human stress.

> *"The proof is in the animal healing, because there is no placebo effect with animals like there can be with humans."*
>
> Rose De Dan
> healer

So what are all these types of healing and do they really work?

Reiki is a noninvasive form of energy healing facilitated by the practitioner to assist the client in creating balance—emotionally, physically, mentally, and spiritually.

"Similar to the way our blood circulates, we also have pathways of energy circulation," describes De Dan. "We're more than just physical bodies. We have energy bodies and spirit bodies as well."

The Chinese call this energy our vital force or "qi" and the Japanese call it "ki." Hence the name "Rei-ki" which means the sacred, vital force.

Shamanic healing, on the other hand, is just it like sounds—traditional healing by an indigenous shaman. Considered an urban shaman, De Dan was trained by the Q'ero people's own "pacos" (or shaman) from Peru.

"It's an animistic belief system that all things have spirit," she explains. "We use a mesa—a bundle of healing stones—to track energy blockages and re-establish energy flow."

As for Acutonics®, a practice developed by acupuncturists, it combines music theory with the knowledge of acupuncture to stimulate energy points via specially calibrated tuning forks. And it works!

"The proof is in the animal healing," De Dan explains. "Because there is no placebo effect with animals like there can be with humans, you know it works. A geriatric dog can come in here barely able to walk up the stairs, but after a session or two will show increased mobility. You can see the results."

Common animal issues De Dan helps treat include things like injuries, eating disorders, stress, and the end stages of life.

Raised in South Jersey, De Dan grew up in a house full of animals with a mother who rescued injured or abandoned critters.

"We were the only people in suburbia with diving ducks in the bathtub and a South American chicken on the patio," she reflects.

De Dan was a graphic designer for years when she was turned on to taking a Reiki class.

What:
Healing for Pets and Humans

Where:
Wild Reiki and Shamanic Healing
(call for directions)
www.reikishamanic.com
206.933.7877

When:
Call for appointments

Price:
Prices vary with treatments and classes; inquire within

"It was like the universe tapped me on the shoulder and said, 'Hey, you need to be a healer,'" she beams. "It was like Christmas—getting some huge surprise present that I didn't know I really wanted."

Reiki was her doorway to all other forms of healing, and she's been training and practicing ever since.

So if you or your pet want to give the wilder side of treatments a try, step into De Dan's office and experience the healing.

100 | *Indoor Adventure at Capers*

Say the word "capers" to any West Seattleite, and most would think of their neighborhood store well before associating the term with a lively adventure, let alone a small, marinated pea-like vegetable.

But according to owner Lisa Myers, it is all these things.

"Capers is an indoor adventure—in food, shopping, and fun," she smiles.

Myers purchased the kitchen store, originally called Sorel's, in 1985. Soon after, the store moved north two doors, and she changed the name to Capers (which was a caper in itself).

> **"Capers is an indoor adventure—in food, shopping, and fun."**
>
> Lisa Myers
> owner

"I sat down with five dictionaries—this was before the Internet, mind you—and searched and searched for a name, but with very specific criteria in mind," describes Myers. "The word had to have a strong sound, a relation to food without getting tied to a certain ethnicity, and a hint at being slightly gourmet but not too fancy. It also had to be easy to pronounce and write on a check—something customer-friendly."

When she came across "caper," with the double meaning of adventure and a gourmet food, Myers knew she'd found a name as well as a vision for her store.

"We make every part of the experience here an adventure," she says.

Just walk in the old wood-framed doors, and the adventure begins. You can brave a flavorful escapade when you sink your teeth into the savory Aunt Pat signature sandwich, prepared with black pepper chicken, gorgonzola cream cheese, mango chutney, and pear slices on toasted Italian Como bread. Or quest for one of the best little lattes in the West with a cup of locally roasted Zoka coffee. Venture to find the perfect leather ottoman for your condo or journey to the jewelry counter to

ENRICHMENT

discover a gem of a selection by local artist Susan Goodwin. The wee ones can also open up a world of adventure with one of many colorful, creative children's books.

"Anyone at any age can come in and take part," Myers explains. "And sure, we have nice things, but it's casual here. People bring their dogs, kids come play in the toy department, and parents get coffee and shop around."

And when it comes to the concept of the 'third place'—the place people choose to go other than work or home—Capers ranks number three for many West Seattleites.

"Friends meet here for coffee, families come here after church, moms bring their babies," says Myers.

In fact, it's been a neighborhood gathering place for more than 20 years. Myers is pleasantly surprised with its generational influence. "I didn't realize how established we were until the same kids that used to come in strollers with their parents years before are now applying for jobs and wanting to work here."

More than just a store, Capers is part of an already tight-knit community that somehow seems to bring people together even more.

What:
Indoor Adventure at Capers

Where:
4521 California Ave SW
www.capershome.com
206.932.0371

When:
Monday–Friday 7 am–8 pm
Saturday 8 am–6 pm
Sunday 8 am–5 pm

Price:
Prices vary, inquire within

101 | *Learn to Grow at In Bloom*

Whether you're a serious green thumb or a beginning gardener, there's always room to grow. At In Bloom Home & Garden on the north end of the Junction, owners Pamela Wilkins and Bonita Corliss teach West Seattle how to do just that.

Offering easy-care plants, indoor gardening accessories, gifts, and gardening workshops, In Bloom encourages customers to let nature nurture all aspects of their lives. How did In Bloom begin? By taking root in dreams during a time of loss.

> *"We think you should enjoy playing with gardening, learning about it. Our mantra is: learn, create, grow."*
>
> Pamela Wilkins
> co-owner

After nearly two decades as a librarian for the Seattle Public Library, Corliss was laid off from what she considered her life's calling. Just a few months later, Wilkins, also a librarian, unexpectedly lost her mother, who was her best friend.

The two were forced to look at life from a new perspective and decided to take what many would consider negative blows and turn them into a growing experience—not just for themselves but for all of those around them.

A West Seattle native, Corliss reacquainted herself with the Junction and its new wave of growth. Wilkins, who still works as a librarian at South Seattle Community College, set her sights on doing something fun in addition to her full-time career.

"This really made me realize how short life is," she reflects. "And if there's something you want to do, you should just do it."

Together the two created In Bloom and have been growing ever since.

But why a garden store?

"I love gardening and always have, but I was what you call 'gardening impaired,'" explains Wilkins. "We think you should enjoy playing with gardening, learning about it. Our mantra is: learn, create, grow."

In Bloom even offers a plant-killer support group, where gardeners can come and confess their plant-care problems and begin to grow again. But that's just a taste of In Bloom's crack at creative education.

In fact, the two women have incorporated their backgrounds as librarians to become better plant educators.

In Bloom offers popular workshops each month. They also help you pick out unique plants you can't find anywhere else.

The shop also features garden-related consignment pieces from several local artists like handmade jewelry, garden art, copper bird feeders, and handmade beeswax candles.

"We offer things to help sustain the human spirit," says Corliss. "Whether you choose a custom-made paving stone, a vintage vase, or a live plant, it's about nurturing the self and your friends and family.

"One of the definitions of gardening is 'to cultivate pleasure,'" she smiles. "And that's what we do here."

To learn more about gardening (and love it), plant yourself at In Bloom.

What:
In Bloom Urban Garden Store

Where:
4437 California Ave.
www.inbloomseattle.com
206.932.2588

When:
Monday–Saturday 10 am–6 pm
Sunday 11am–4 pm
(call for holiday & summer hours)

Price:
Free to look, plants and gifts vary